PASSWORD 2

A Reading and Vocabulary Text

Linda Butler

Holyoke Community College

PEARSON
Longman

Dedicato ai miei amici in Italia con un abbraccio

Password 2

Pearson Education, 10 Bank Street, White Plains, NY 10606

Vice President of Multimedia and Skills: Sherry Preiss
Executive editor: Laura Le Dréan
Senior development editor: Joan Poole
Development editor: Mykan White
Production editor: Andréa C. Basora
Vice president of domestic marketing: Kate McLoughlin
Vice president of international marketing: Bruno Paul
Senior manufacturing buyer: Dave Dickey
Photo research: Dana Klinek
Cover design: Tracey Cataldo
Text design: Ann France, Patricia Woszyk
Text composition: Elm Street Publishing Services, Inc.
Text font: 11/13 Palatino
Photo credits: See p. xiii
Illustration credits: Jill Wood pp. 3, 7, 17, 18, 19, 22, 23, 40, 41, 48, 57, 64, 65, 78, 79, 80, 82, 87, 95, 121, 133, 130, 158, 159, 166, 170, 174, 175, 184, 198, 199, 206, 208, 211, 215, 216, 224, 225; Hilary Price pp. 13, 42, 55, 63, 80, 86, 97, 139, 157, 165, 168, 185, 200, 223
Dictionary entries from *Longman Dictionary of American English*

Library of Congress Cataloging-in-Publication Data

Butler, Linda, 1952-
    Password 2: a reading and vocabulary text / by Linda Butler.
      p. cm.
    Includes index.
    ISBN 0-13-048467-9 (pbk.) —ISBN 0-13-140892-5 (pbk : CD)
    1. English language—Textbooks for foreign speakers. 2. Reading comprehension—Problems, exercises, etc.
  3. Vocabulary—Problems, exercises, etc. I. Title: Password two. II. Title.
    PE1128.B8615 2003
    428.6'4—dc22

                                                   2003021632

ISBN: 0-13-048467-9   6 7 8 9 -CRK- 08
ISBN: 0-13-140892-5 (book with audio CD)   6 7 8 9 -CRK- 07

Printed in the United States of America

Contents

Scope and Sequence

UNIT / CHAPTER / READING	READING SKILLS	VOCABULARY BUILDING	DICTIONARY SKILLS
UNIT 1: STARTING OUT IN A CAREER			
CHAPTER 1 *A Dentist?* *Oh, No!*	• Scanning • Thinking about the main idea	• Guessing meaning from context • Studying parts of speech: nouns (common and proper)	
CHAPTER 2 *A Cool Job*	• Reading for details • Summarizing	• Studying collocations: *pay attention*	
CHAPTER 3 *Ready for Action*	• Scanning • Reading between the lines	• Studying parts of speech: verbs	
CHAPTER 4 *Life Is Full of Surprises*	• Reading for details • Understanding cause and effect	• Studying phrasal verbs	
UNIT 1: Wrap-up		• Expanding vocabulary: adjectives; word families	• Using guidewords • Finding compound words and phrasal verbs
UNIT 2: IT'S ALL IN YOUR HEAD			
CHAPTER 5 *Food for Thought*	• Scanning • Thinking about the main idea	• Studying collocations: adjective + *amount (of)*	
CHAPTER 6 *Your Memory at Work*	• Understanding topics of paragraphs • Summarizing	• Studying parts of speech: adverbs	
CHAPTER 7 *Sleep and the Brain*	• Reading for details • Summarizing	• Studying word grammar: *affect, effect*	
CHAPTER 8 *In Your Dreams*	• Distinguishing between fact and opinion • Summarizing	• Studying collocations: phrases with *right*	
UNIT 2: Wrap-up		• Expanding vocabulary: prefixes and suffixes	• Finding adverbs that end in *-ly* • Understanding word families

About the Author

Linda Butler is an independent ESL materials writer and editor and the author of several textbooks for learners of English, including *Password 1*. She began teaching English in Italy in 1979 and currently teaches part-time at Holyoke Community College in Massachusetts.

INTRODUCTION

To the Teacher

The *Password* series is designed to help learners of English develop their reading skills and expand their vocabularies. Each book in the series offers theme-based units with engaging readings, a variety of activities to develop language skills, and exercises to help students understand, remember, and use new words.

Any book in the series can be used independently of the others. *Password 1* is for high beginners assumed to have an English vocabulary of about 600 words; *Password 2* assumes a vocabulary of about 1,000 words; and *Password 3*, assumes a vocabulary of about 1,500. With each book, students will learn more than 400 new words and phrases, all of them high-frequency in American English. The *Password* series can help students reach the 2,000-word level in English, at which point, research has shown, most learners can handle basic everyday oral communication and begin to read unadapted texts. The vocabulary taught in the *Password* series has been carefully chosen. Target word choices have been based on analyses of authentic language data in various corpora, including data in the Longman Corpus Network, to determine which words are most frequently used and therefore most likely to be needed by students. Also targeted are common collocations and other multi-word units, including phrasal verbs. Most of the target vocabulary has been determined not by the topic of a chapter but rather by the frequency and usefulness of the words across a range of subjects.

While becoming a good reader in English does involve more than knowing the meanings of words, there is no doubt that vocabulary is key. To learn new words, students need to see them repeatedly and in varied contexts. They must become skilled at guessing meaning from context but can do this successfully only when they understand the context. For that reason, the sentence structure and vocabulary in the readings have been carefully controlled. The vocabulary used in the readings is limited to those 600 or 1,000 or 1,500 high-frequency words that the learner is assumed to know, plus the words and phrases to be targeted in the chapter and those recycled from previous chapters. The new vocabulary is explained and practiced in exercises and activities, encountered again in later readings and tasks, and reviewed in oral drills and self-tests. This emphasis on systematic vocabulary acquisition is a highlight of the *Password* series.

OVERVIEW OF *PASSWORD 2*

Password 2 is intended for low-intermediate students. It assumes a vocabulary of about 1,000 English words and teaches about 400 more. Sixteen words and phrases from each reading passage are targeted in the exercises for that chapter and recycled in later chapters. Because of the systematic building of vocabulary, as well as the progression of reading skills exercises, it is best to do the units and chapters in the order in which they appear in the book.

Most of the target words are among the 1,500 most high-frequency words in English—the vocabulary that students need to build a solid foundation in English. Other less high-frequency words have been targeted for their usefulness in discussing a particular theme. For example, the first unit, "Starting Out in a Career," includes the target words *career, boss, training*, and *interview*.

Organization of the Book

The book contains six units, each with four chapters followed by a Wrap-up section. After Units Three and Six, there are Vocabulary Self-Tests. At the end of the book, you will find the Index to Target Words and Phrases.

UNITS   Each unit is based on a theme and includes four readings that deal with real people, places, ideas, and events. Students need to understand the content, they need to speak and write about it, but they are not expected to memorize it. Each of the readings and each list of target vocabulary has been recorded on audio CD.

CHAPTERS   Each of the four chapters within a unit is organized as follows:

Getting Ready to Read   Each chapter opens with a photo or illustration and pre-reading questions or tasks. These are often for pair or small group work but may be best handled as a full-class activity when students need more guidance. *Getting Ready to Read* starts students thinking about the subject of the reading by drawing on what they already know, eliciting their opinions, and/or introducing relevant vocabulary.

Reading   This section contains the reading passage for the chapter. These passages progress from about 450 to about 750 words by the end of the book. Students should do the reading the first time without dictionaries. You may wish to have them reread while you read aloud or play the audio, as listening while reading can be helpful to students' comprehension and retention. It is also helpful for students to hear the pronunciation of new words. The reading is followed by *Quick Comprehension Check,* a brief true/false exercise that lets students check their general understanding. It is a good idea to go over the *Quick Comprehension Check* statements in class. When a statement is true, you may want to ask students how they know it is true; when it is false, have students correct it. By doing so, you send them back into the reading to find support for their answers. Try to avoid spending time explaining vocabulary at this point.

Exploring Vocabulary   Once students have a general understanding of the reading, it is time to focus on new words. In *Thinking about the Vocabulary*, students are asked to look at the list of Target Words and Phrases and circle (both on the list and in the reading) those that are new to them. Then they reread, noticing the uses of these particular words. From the beginning, learners are asked to examine the context of each unknown word and see what information the context gives them. They may need to work on this first as a whole class, with your guidance; later they can discuss new word meanings in pairs. *Using the Vocabulary* follows, with three exercises of various types, to help students understand the meanings of the target vocabulary as used in the reading and in other contexts. These exercises can be done in class or out, by students working individually or in pairs. In *Building on the Vocabulary*, you will find a word grammar or collocation exercise. Grammar exercises include study of the most common parts of speech and phrasal verbs. The collocation exercises focus students' attention on how words combine with others, given that knowing about possible word combinations is an important aspect of learning new vocabulary. For example, students will see that *make*, not *do* or *give*, goes with *an effort*, and that while *gain, earn,* and *win* may be similar in meaning, they combine with different nouns. Only after working through all the exercises in *Exploring Vocabulary* should students turn to their dictionaries for further information, if needed.

Developing Your Skills   In this section are tasks that require students to focus again on the reading. The exercises include work on scanning, answering comprehension questions, summarizing, understanding cause and effect, reading for details, paraphrasing and quoting, comparing and contrasting, using context clues, and stating the main idea. You will also find a fluency-building exercise: *Discussion, Sharing Opinions, Role-playing,* or *Interviewing*. The exercise *Using New Words* has pairs of students working productively with the target vocabulary orally and/or in writing. When students choose new words to use in sentences, encourage them to choose ones they need to learn more about. The chapter ends with *Writing*. Sometimes there will be a choice of two or more topics related to the content of the reading. These writing tasks may lend themselves to journal entries or more formal compositions. How you wish to use them will depend on your goals for the course.

UNIT WRAP-UPS   Each unit ends with a four-part Wrap-up section that brings together the vocabulary from the four chapters. The unit Wrap-up provides a key follow-up to the initial learning of the vocabulary—to consolidate and enrich students' understanding of new words. The first part is *Reviewing Vocabulary*, with varied exercises to review word meanings; the second is *Expanding Vocabulary*, with exercises on word families, word parts, and collocations; the third is *Playing with Words*, a crossword or word search puzzle; and the fourth is *Building Dictionary Skills*, using excerpts from *Longman Dictionary of American English*.

VOCABULARY SELF-TESTS   Two multiple choice vocabulary tests appear in the book, the first covering Units 1–3, the second Units 4–6. The answers are given at the back of the book, as these are intended for students' own use. (Unit tests can be found in the Teacher's Manual.)

TEACHER'S MANUAL

The Teacher's Manual for *Password 2* contains:

- The Answer Key for all exercises in the book
- Six Unit Tests with answers
- *Quick Oral Review,* sets of prompts you can use for rapid drills of vocabulary studied in previous chapters. These drills can be an important part of the spaced repetition of vocabulary—repeated exposures to newly-learned words at increasing intervals—that helps students remember the words they learn. For tips on how to use the prompts, see the Introduction in the Teacher's Manual.

To the Student

Welcome to *Password 2!* This book will help you improve your reading in English and expand your English vocabulary. The articles in it are about real people, events, ideas, and places from around the world. I hope you will enjoy reading, writing, and talking about them.

Linda Butler

References

Nation, Paul. *Teaching and Learning Vocabulary*. New York: Newbury House, 1990.

Schmitt, Norbert, and Michael McCarthy, eds. *Vocabulary: Description, Acquisition, and Pedagogy*. Cambridge, UK: Cambridge University Press, 1997.

Schmitt, Norbert, and Cheryl Boyd Zimmerman. "Derivative Word Forms: What Do Learners Know?" *TESOL Quarterly*, 36 (Summer 2002): 145–171.

Acknowledgments

I would like to thank first the people who shared personal stories with me so that students could enjoy them in this book: Mahmoud Arani, Kazumi Funamoto, Charles Lane, Brandon Middleton, Stephen Roy, and Bruce Yang. For their help with research, I would like to thank Craig Butler, Maggie Butler, Vitek J.P. Kruta, Siok Kuan Lim, Jim Montgomery, Miles and Clare Montgomery-Butler, Gail Mueller, Beatrice Romano, and Lynn Stafford-Yilmaz. Thanks also to my students at Holyoke Community College in Holyoke, Massachusetts, for their helpful feedback on the materials, especially to Julissa Garib and Lisandra Zeno, for the use of excerpts from their journals, and to readers Mayra Colón, Catherine López, Nasir Maqbool, Mónica Pérez, Jocelyn Sanchez, Luz Serrano, and Tatyana Skovorodina.

I would also like to thank the reviewers whose comments on early drafts of this book were very helpful: **Marsha Abramovich**, Tidewater Community College, Virginia Beach, VA; **Allan Aube**, Canadian Education Centre, Seoul, Korea; **Kathy Burns**, EF International Language School, Miami, FL; **Leslie Corpuz**, Tidewater Community College, Virginia Beach, VA; **William W. Crawford**, Georgetown University, Washington, D.C.; **Laura Freeman**, Oedae Language School, Kyonggi-Do, South Korea; **Elena Lattarulo**, Cuesta College, San Luis Obispo, CA; **Craig Machado**, Norwalk Community College, Norwalk, CT; **Denise Selleck**, City College of San Francisco–Alemany, San Francisco, CA.

A great many people at Longman helped in the making of this book, most of all Executive Editor Laura Le Dréan. Her experience as an editor and as a teacher, her good judgment and good humor, and her unfailing support were invaluable. I would also like to thank Assistant Editor Dana Klinek, Development Editors Joan Poole and Mykan White, Production Editor Andréa C. Basora, and artists Hilary Price and Jill Wood.

Photo Credits

p. 1, © Ted Horowitz/Corbis; p. 2, Photo by Linda Butler; p. 10, Photo by Linda Butler; p. 18, © Reuters NewMedia, Inc./Corbis; p. 26, Photo by Karl Sklar; p. 38, © Dale O'Dell/Corbis; p. 39, © John Henley/Corbis; p. 47, © Jose Luis Pelaez, Inc./Corbis; p. 76, © Carol Kohen/Getty Images; p. 77, © Royalty-Free/Corbis; p. 94, © Bettmann/Corbis; p. 102, © Stanley Fellerman/Corbis; p. 119, © Herrmann/Starke/Corbis; p. 120, Photo courtesy of Bruce Yang; p. 128, © Andrew Holbrooke; p. 136, Photo by Nancy Carbonaro, Carbonaro Photography, Wellesley, MA; p. 144, © H. Prinz/corbisstockmarket.com; p. 156, © Duncan Smith/Getty Images; p. 173, left: © Firefly Productions/Corbis; top right: © Myrleen Ferguson Cate/PhotoEdit; bottom right: © George Obremski/Corbis; p. 182, © Patrick Darby/Corbis; p. 196, © Ed Honowitz/Getty Images; p. 197, National Institute of Standards and Technology, Boulder Laboratories, U.S. Department of Commerce; p. 206, © Massimo Mastrorillo/Corbis; p. 214, © Photo by JC Bourque; p. 223, © Forrest J. Ackerman Collection/Corbis

UNIT 1

STARTING OUT IN A CAREER

CHAPTER 1

A Dentist? Oh, No!

Dr. Kazumi Funamoto, dentist

GETTING READY TO READ

Talk with a partner or in a small group.

1. How often do you go to the dentist?
2. How do you feel about going to the dentist?
3. How many years of schooling does a dentist need?
4. Is being a dentist a good job? Tell why or why not.

READING

Look at the words and pictures next to the reading. Then read without stopping. Don't worry about new words. Don't stop to use a dictionary. Just keep reading!

A Dentist? Oh, No!

1   When people ask Kazumi Funamoto, "**What do you do?**" she answers, "I'm a dentist." Then she watches for the look on their faces. The same thing almost always happens. She can see that they are thinking, "I don't like dentists." She understands how they feel. They are thinking about **needles** and drills[1] and pain.

2   Kazumi does not want her patients to be afraid. She takes time to talk to them and ease[2] their **fears**. She tells them, "It's going to be OK. I'm going to be as **gentle** as I can. I don't like pain myself!" She always explains what she is going to do. She helps her patients feel **calm** and **relaxed**.

3   When she was a child, Kazumi did not like going to the dentist. She never expected to become one herself. She used to think about becoming an interpreter.[3] She was **interested** in other languages, and she liked talking to people from other countries. Kazumi chose a different **career**, but **communication** is still a big part of her job. She needs to talk with her patients and with the people who work in her office. They need to understand each other well.

4   Growing up, Kazumi talked about careers with her aunt. She says, "My aunt was a medical technician,[4] and she had a big **influence** on me." This aunt sometimes took Kazumi to work with her. Kazumi liked being in the lab.[5] There were doctors and technicians working there. She liked watching and listening to them.

5   In college, Kazumi had to get braces[6] on her teeth. "That was no fun, but the results were wonderful!" she says. Then she started to think about becoming a dentist. So, she spent some time helping in a dentist's office. She learned what a dentist's job was like. This experience helped her **make up her mind**. She decided to go to dental school after college.

6   Today, Kazumi feels great about her career. She gives three reasons why she is glad to be a dentist. First of all, she

continued

[1] a dentist's *drill*

[2] *ease* = make (a problem) smaller or not so bad

[3] an *interpreter* = a person who repeats someone's words in another language

[4] a *medical technician* = a worker who knows how to use machines or do tests that help doctors

[5] a *lab* = (short for) a *laboratory,* a room where scientists do careful tests

[6] *braces*

knows that she makes her mother happy. Her mother is glad that Kazumi can **support** herself. She told her daughter, "You won't have to depend on a husband. Good for you!"[7] Kazumi also likes working with her hands. A dentist needs a gentle touch and great control of very small **movements.** "I think I have good hands for this kind of work," she says. Finally, she likes learning new things. As a dentist, she learns from experience and from talking with her **boss.** At the end of the day, they often talk about difficult **cases.** She asks him questions about problems that **come up** with her patients' teeth, and she gets his advice. Kazumi says, "I feel like I'm growing each and every day."

[7] *Good for you!* = said to show you are happy about something that someone did

Quick Comprehension Check

Read these sentences. Circle T (true) or F (false).

1. All her life, Kazumi Funamoto wanted to be a dentist.   T   (F)

2. She doesn't usually talk to her patients.   T   F

3. She used to go to work with her aunt.   T   F

4. Kazumi's mother is happy that Kazumi is a dentist.   T   F

5. Kazumi works alone.   T   F

6. She is happy to be a dentist.   T   F

EXPLORING VOCABULARY

Thinking about the Vocabulary

Guessing Meaning from Context

We use words in a **context.** The context of a word is the words and sentences before and after it. These other words help you guess a word's meaning. For example, look at the context of *boss*:

> As a dentist, she learns from experience and from talking with her **boss.** At the end of the day, they often talk about difficult cases. She can ask him questions about problems that come up with her patients' teeth, and she gets his advice.

The context of *boss* tells you this is a person and it is someone at work. A boss can answer questions and give advice. *Boss* means the person who gives someone a job or tells a worker what to do.

Look at the target words and phrases. Which ones are new to you? Circle them here and in the reading.

Target Words and Phrases

What do you do? (paragraph 1)	**interested** (3)	**support** (6)
needles (1)	**career** (3)	**movements** (6)
fears (2)	**communication** (3)	**boss** (6)
gentle (2)	**influence** (4)	**cases** (6)
calm (2)	**make up her mind** (5)	**come up** (6)
relaxed (2)		

Read "A Dentist? Oh, No!" again. Look at the context of each new word and phrase. Can you guess the meaning?

Using the Vocabulary

 These sentences are **about the reading**. Complete them with the words and phrases in the box.

career	cases	come up	~~fear~~	gentle	influence
interested in	make up her mind	movements	relaxed	support	

1. Many people have a _____fear_____ of dentists. They are afraid of going to see a dentist.

2. Kazumi says, "I'm going to be as _____ as I can." This means she will be very careful in the way she touches her patient.

3. She doesn't want her patients to be nervous. She wants them to feel

   _____.

4. Kazumi liked learning about other languages. She was _____ them.

5. First she thought about a _____ as an interpreter. Then she decided on a different kind of work.

6. Kazumi learned from her aunt while she was growing up. Her aunt had a big _____ on her.

7. After college, Kazumi needed to decide on a career. She had to

   _____.

8. As a dentist, she makes enough money to live. She can _____ herself.

9. When Kazumi's hands are in a patient's mouth, she needs to move them carefully. She has to use very small _____.

10. Sometimes patients have special problems with their teeth. Kazumi talks about these difficult _____ with her boss.

11. "Problems that _____" are problems that happen, often suddenly, when someone isn't ready for them.

B These sentences use the target words and phrases **in new contexts.** Complete them with the words and phrases in the box.

came up	career	cases	fear	gentle	influence
interested in	made up my mind	~~movements~~	relaxed	support	

1. The doctor tested the ___movements___ of my eyes: up, down, left, and right.

2. He needs a job so that he can _____ himself and his family.

3. They're lying on the beach listening to music. They look very _____.

4. He had a 50-year-long _____ in business.

5. I like the new president. He'll have a good _____ on the country.

6. They aren't _____ money. They don't care about it.

7. It was hard to choose which shoes to buy, but finally I _____.

8. He planned to leave work early, but something _____, so he couldn't.

9. Be careful with the baby! You must be _____ with babies.

10. _____ of flying is common. Many people won't get on a plane.

11. In some _____, the dentist has to pull a tooth out, but sometimes the dentist can save a tooth.

C Read these sentences. Write the **boldfaced** target words or phrases next to their definitions.

a. A family needs good **communication**. People have to talk to each other.

b. You work for the college, right? **What do you do?** Do you teach?

c. Police and firefighters must stay **calm** so that they can think clearly.

d. A doctor uses a **needle** to give someone a shot of medicine or a drug.

e. The **boss** let the workers leave early.

Target Words/Phrases   Definitions

1. _____*boss*_____ = the person who gives you a job or tells you what to do

2. _____ = What is your job?

3. _____ = a very thin piece of steel

4. _____ = relaxed, not angry or nervous

5. _____ = giving and getting information (by speaking, writing, and so on)

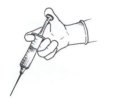

A syringe with a *needle*

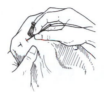

A sewing *needle*

Building on the Vocabulary

Studying Word Grammar

The **parts of speech** are the different kinds of words, such as nouns, verbs, and adjectives. A **noun** is a word for:

a person	*dentist, aunt, Kazumi*
a place	*home, school, Africa*
a thing	*tooth, book, Volkswagen*
an idea	*time, education, music*

Most nouns are **common nouns** (such as *dentist, home, tooth*). A **proper noun** starts with a capital letter and names one special person (*Kazumi*), place (*Africa*), or thing (*Volkswagen*).

A There are one, two, or three nouns in each sentence. Circle the nouns.

1. She has good communication with the players on her team.

2. Are you afraid of needles?

3. The police are working on a difficult case.

4. The boss is moving into a new office.

5. Did his family have an influence on his career?

6. John is going to the airport by bus.

7. My friend is in Australia right now.

Write the nouns from Part A. Some nouns can go in more than one place.

Nouns are words for:

People	Places	Things	Ideas
players		team	communication

DEVELOPING YOUR SKILLS

Scanning

Sometimes you need to find a piece of information in a reading. To do this, you **scan** the reading. *Scan* means to read very quickly and look for just the information you need.

Read these statements about "A Dentist? Oh, No!" Scan the reading for the information you need to complete them.

1. Kazumi tells her patients, "I'm going to _____ <u>be as gentle as I can</u> _____."

2. Kazumi also thought about a career as an _____.

3. Communication is important in her work. She needs to talk with

    _____ and _____.

4. Kazumi had two experiences that helped her decide on a career as a

    dentist: first, _____; then, _____.

5. Kazumi gives three reasons for liking her work: **a.** _____,

    b. _____, and

    c. _____.

Thinking about the Main Idea

 A reading is about someone or something. That person or thing is the **topic** of the reading.

What is the topic of "A Dentist? Oh, No!"? Circle 1, 2, or 3.

1. Going to the dentist

2. A dentist and her family

3. Kazumi Funamoto and her career

B The **main idea** of a reading is the most important information about the topic.

What is the main idea of the reading in this chapter? Circle 1, 2, or 3.

1. Kazumi Funamoto knows that people don't like to go to the dentist.
2. A dentist needs to have good hands and a gentle touch to help patients stay calm.
3. Kazumi Funamoto didn't always plan to be a dentist, but now she is happy in that career.

Discussion

Talk about these questions with a partner.

1. How did Kazumi's aunt have an influence on her?
2. Who had the biggest influence on you when you were a child? Who has an influence on you now?
3. Name five to ten jobs in which a person works with his or her hands. Would you like any of these jobs? Explain.

Using New Words

These questions use some of the target words and phrases. Ask and answer these questions with a partner. Then tell the class something about your partner.

1. Is it sometimes hard for you to **make up your mind**? When?
2. When you pick up a newspaper or magazine, what are you **interested in**?
3. Would you like a **career** as a dentist? Why or why not?
4. How would you finish this sentence? A good **boss** is a person who . . .
5. What do you do to stay **calm** and **relaxed** at difficult moments?

Writing

Write a paragraph about a time when you had to make an important decision. Answer these questions:

- What did you decide? Why?
- Did anyone have an influence on your decision?
- How do you feel about your decision now?

Example:

My big decision in life was to come to the United States with my family. My husband and I made this decision together. We wanted to do it for our children. It wasn't easy because we had no other family here. Now I am glad we came.

CHAPTER 2

A Cool Job

Charles Lane

GETTING READY TO READ

Talk in a small group or with the whole class.

1. What video games can you name?

2. Do you ever play video games? Tell why or why not.

3. Charles Lane works for a video game company. His first experience in this area was working as a video game tester. Does this sound like a good job for you or anyone you know? Tell why or why not.

READING

Look at the words next to the reading. Then read without stopping.

A Cool Job

1   Charles Lane loves playing games, all kinds of games. He has loved games all his life. He has always been interested in computers, too. Today, his love of games and his interest in computers come together in his work. Charles works for a company that makes video games.

2   Charles did not really plan on this career. "It all started **by accident**," he says. "A friend of a friend worked for a video game company. He knew how much I loved games, and he told me about a job. It sounded like fun." It was a job as a video game tester.

3   When a video game company has a new game, they give it to testers. Testers play the game and look for bugs in it. The word *bug* usually means an **insect**, but a bug can also be a problem in a computer program. "For example," says Charles, "you're playing a war game, and you're flying a plane. You drop a **bomb** on a building, but nothing happens—the building is still standing. The bomb didn't work, so you know there's a bug." The company wants to find and fix any bugs before they sell the game.

4   Video game testers need to have good computer **skills**. They need to understand how computers work. They have to install[1] new **hardware** and **software**. Charles did not have great computer skills when he went to the **interview** for his first job, so he was nervous. **However**, the interviewer said, "That's OK. We can teach someone to use a computer, but we can't teach someone to love games."

5   Testers must have strong communication skills, too. They have to write very clear **reports** on the bugs they find. They have to describe **exactly** what is wrong in a game. Oral[2] communication skills are important, too. Testers are part of a team. Every day, they talk with other people on the team, such as the game designers[3] and programmers.[4] They all want to make their game fun and easy to use.

[1] *install* = put in place and make ready to use

[2] *oral* = spoken, not written

[3] *designers* = people who plan what things will look like and how they will work

[4] *programmers* = people who write computer programs (the instructions that make computers do their jobs)

continued

6   In his first job as a tester, Charles sometimes had to check **certain** parts of a game. At other times, he just started at the beginning and played the game, looking for bugs. He tried to **imagine** all the things that a player at home might do in a game. He played hour after hour, day after day. He always had to **pay attention** to **details**. Did he ever get tired of playing? "You bet!"[5] says Charles. "After 60 hours of testing in a week, you do not want to play games when you get home."

7   Charles spent three years as a video game tester. Now he is a video game producer. This means that he works on every part of **developing** a new game. He really enjoys his work. Charles says, "It's a great **field** to be in."

[5] *You bet! = (informal) a strong yes*

Quick Comprehension Check

Read these sentences. Circle T (true) or F (false).

1. Charles always planned to work for a video game company. T F
2. Testers check new games to look for any problems. T F
3. Testers need to know something about computers. T F
4. Testers don't need to be good writers or speakers. T F
5. It usually takes a team of people to make a new video game. T F
6. Charles wants to change to a different career. T F

EXPLORING VOCABULARY

Thinking about the Vocabulary

Look at the target words and phrases. Which ones are new to you? Circle them here and in the reading.

Target Words and Phrases			
by accident (2)	hardware (4)	reports (5)	pay attention (6)
insect (3)	software (4)	exactly (5)	details (6)
bomb (3)	interview (4)	certain (6)	developing (7)
skills (4)	however (4)	imagine (6)	field (7)

Read "A Cool Job" again. Look at the context of each new word and phrase. Can you guess the meaning?

Using the Vocabulary

A Label the pictures. Write *a bomb, computer hardware, insects,* and *an interview.*

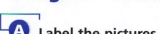

1. _____

2. _____

3. _____

4. _____

B These sentences are **about the reading.** Complete them with the words and phrases in the box.

by accident	certain	details	develop	exactly	field
however	imagine	pay attention	report	skills	software

1. Charles's career in video games started _____. He didn't plan on it.

2. Video game testers need to know how to use computers. They need computer _____. Charles developed these abilities at his first job.

3. Testers sometimes have to install computer _____. These programs tell a computer what to do.

4. Charles didn't have great computer skills, so he was nervous at his interview. _____, his interviewer said, "Don't worry."

5. A tester has to tell people at the company about the bugs in a game. The tester writes about the problems in a _____.

6. Testers have to describe a bug _____. They have to tell every little thing about it.

7. Sometimes Charles didn't test all of a game. He tested _____ parts only.

8. Charles thought about game players at home. He pictured them in his mind. He tried to _____ everything they might do in a game.

9. You can't think about other things when you test a game. You have to _____ to the game.

10. Testers look at every little part of a game. They pay attention to _____.

11. It takes a team of people to _____ a new video game. It is hard for one person working alone to make a good game.

12. Charles likes the video game business. He says it is a great _____ to work in.

C These sentences use the target words and phrases **in new contexts. Complete them with the words and phrases in the box.**

by accident	certain	details	developing	exactly	field
however	imagine	pays attention	report	skills	software

1. I wonder if it will rain. Let's watch the weather _____ on TV.

2. You need good driving _____ to pass the test for a driver's license.

3. I didn't expect to see her. We met _____.

4. The boss bought some new _____ for use on the office computers.

5. I remember something about the case, but I forget the _____.

6. Bob gets bad grades in school. He never _____ in class.

7. Scientists are _____ new drugs to fight AIDS.

8. What time is it? It is _____ 4:31.

9. Close your eyes, relax, and _____ lying on a beautiful beach.

10. He has classes on _____ days. I don't know which ones.

11. I expected her to be angry. _____, she seemed very calm.

12. Teachers work in the _____ of education. (This target word can also mean an area of land used for playing a sport, planting vegetables, **etc.**)

Common Abbreviations

Etc. is short for the Latin words *et cetera.* This abbreviation is often used at the end of a list. It means "and other people or things of the same kind."

Building on the Vocabulary

Studying Collocations

Collocations are words that we often put together. Some words can go together and some cannot. For example, we can say, *He never **pays** attention,* but we can't say, *He never **gives** attention.*

Note that *pay attention* is often followed by *to* + (someone/something): *Pay attention to your driving!*

Choose the correct sentence. Cross out the sentence with the mistake.

1. The teacher told them to pay attention. / ~~The teacher told them to give attention.~~

2. I gave no attention to the news. / I paid no attention to the news.

3. Please pay careful attention about this. / Please pay careful attention to this.

4. Sorry, I wasn't paying attention. / Sorry, I wasn't giving attention.

DEVELOPING YOUR SKILLS

Reading for Details

Read these sentences. Then reread "A Cool Job" for the answers. If the reading doesn't give the information, check (✓) *It doesn't say.*

	True	False	It doesn't say.
1. Charles loved games when he was a child.	✓		
2. He was interested in computers when he was a boy.			
3. He got his first job with a video game company after reading about the job in the newspaper.			
4. Video game testers need writing skills.			
5. Charles had an interview for his first job as a tester.			
6. He finished college before becoming a tester.			
7. Video game testers look for bugs in games.			
8. They sometimes work more than 50 hours a week.			
9. They make a lot of money.			
10. Charles still works as a video game tester.			

Summarizing

A **summary** tells the important parts of a reading again, but it has only the main ideas, not the details.

A These six sentences make up a summary of the reading. Number the sentences in order.

_____ **a.** They also need good communication skills.

_____ **b.** They need good computer skills and a love of video games.

__1__ **c.** Charles Lane works in the video game business.

_____ **d.** Today, Charles is a video game producer.

_____ **e.** His first job in this field was as a video game tester.

_____ **f.** Testers check new games for bugs.

B Write the sentences from Part A as a paragraph.

_____
_____
_____
_____
_____
_____
_____

Sharing Opinions

Think about the questions. Then talk in a small group.

1. A friend of a friend helped Charles get his first job with a video game company. Some people say, "When you are looking for a job, it's _who_ you know—not _what_ you know—that matters." What does this statement mean? Do you agree with it? Why or why not?

2. Why do video game testers need strong communication skills? What other jobs need these skills? Which of these jobs do you think are good jobs? Why?

Using New Words

Work with a partner. Choose five target words or phrases from the list on page 12. On a piece of paper, use each word or phrase in a sentence.

Writing

Write a paragraph about your first job. Maybe it was a job you had two years ago—or twenty-two. Where did you work, what did you do, and how did you feel about this job? Or maybe your first job is still in your future: When will you get a job, and what would you like to do?

Example:

My first job was in a supermarket. I was 16 years old. I worked there as a cashier. When I started, I didn't like the job because I didn't know anything about cash registers. I felt stupid. But day by day, I learned, and now I know everything about using a cash register.

CHAPTER 3

Ready for Action

A crew of firefighters

GETTING READY TO READ

Talk with a partner or in a small group.

1. Look at the photo. What kind of firefighters do you think these are? What are they doing?

2. Do you carry your books in a backpack?[1] If so, how much does it weigh?

3. How long would it take you to hike[2] three miles? (That would be almost five kilometers.) What about hiking three miles with a 45-pound backpack? (That would weigh about 20 kilograms.)

[1] a *backpack*

[2] *hike* = take a long walk in the country, in the mountains, etc.

READING

Look at the words and pictures next to the reading. Then read without stopping.

Ready for Action

1   When most people leave for work, they know exactly where they are going. They usually know what time they will get home, too. Brandon Middleton never knows for sure. He might **end up** working for eight hours, ten, or sixteen. Maybe he won't even get home that same week. But that is fine with him. It is all part of being a firefighter for the U.S. Forest Service.

2   Fighting **forest** fires is dangerous work. It can also be very exciting. Imagine being out in a forest, far from any city or town. (Maybe you're a "smoke jumper" and you jumped out of a plane to get there!) You are on your way to fight a fire. The air is heavy with the smoke from the burning trees. As you get closer, the sound of the fire fills your ears like the sound of a train rushing **toward** you. You know that **ahead of** you is the fire. It is like a monster[1] that you and your team must **destroy**.

3   Is being a firefighter always exciting? Brandon says no. The first thing he will tell you about the job is, "It's all about **patience**." He and his crew[2] spend a lot of time waiting and a lot of time getting ready. Each one is **in charge of** his or her own equipment.[3] They have to make sure their **tools** are **sharp**. They need to have all the right clothes, such as a helmet,[4] **leather** boots, and fire-resistant[5] pants and shirts. Each firefighter will carry a backpack that weighs 25–45 pounds (12–20 kilograms). Firefighters have to be ready to move quickly. They never know when the phone will ring.

4   Three years ago, Brandon was in college. He wanted a job just for the summer. His mother told him that the Forest Service had some jobs **available**. Brandon loves forests and being **outdoors**, so he decided to **apply** for a job as a firefighter. He did not go back to college that fall.

5   After getting the job, Brandon had to pass a test. He had to do a three-mile hike with a 45-pound pack on his back, and he had to do it in less than 45 minutes. Then he needed

continued

[1] a *monster*

[2] a *crew* = a team of workers

[3] *equipment* = things needed to do a job, play a sport, etc.

[4] a *helmet*

[5] *fire-resistant* = hard to burn

training, so he went to fire school. There he started learning about things like using tools, watching the weather, and staying safe. "But fire school is only one week. The real training is on the job," he says. "That is where all the learning happens—out in the forest. You have to trust the people with more experience, and you learn for yourself as you see more fire."

6   What is next for Brandon? He is thinking about applying for a job on a Hotshot crew. The name *Hotshot* **refers** to working in the hottest area of a forest fire, but *hotshot* also means a person who is very skilled and very confident. Hotshot crews go to all the big fires, and they get the most difficult jobs to do. During the fire **season**, they have to be available 24 hours a day, seven days a week. Not everyone could do this kind of work. Not everyone would want to. "But if this is what you like to do," says Brandon, "you'd love it."

Quick Comprehension Check

Read these sentences. Circle T (true) or F (false).

1. Brandon Middleton loves his work.   T   F

2. He does not work the same hours every day.   T   F

3. Being a firefighter is always exciting.   T   F

4. Firefighters have to carry heavy backpacks.   T   F

5. Brandon learned how to fight fires in college.   T   F

6. He is planning to return to college soon.   T   F

EXPLORING VOCABULARY

Thinking about the Vocabulary

Look at the target words and phrases. Which ones are new to you? Circle them here and in the reading. Then read "Ready for Action" again. Look at the context of each new word and phrase. Can you guess the meaning?

Target Words and Phrases			
end up (1)	**destroy** (2)	**sharp** (3)	**apply** (4)
forest (2)	**patience** (3)	**leather** (3)	**training** (5)
toward (2)	**in charge of** (3)	**available** (4)	**refers** (6)
ahead of (2)	**tools** (3)	**outdoors** (4)	**season** (6)

Using the Vocabulary

A These sentences are about the reading. What is the meaning of each **boldfaced** word or phrase? Circle a, b, or c.

1. Firefighters like Brandon cannot depend on working eight-hour days. They sometimes **end up** working much longer. *End up* means:

   a. make something finish or stop   **b.** like or enjoy something   **c.** have a final result you didn't expect

2. If a fire is moving **toward** you, the sound gets louder. *Toward* means:

   a. because of   **b.** away from   **c.** closer to

3. If a fire is **ahead of** you, you are looking and moving that way. *Ahead of* means:

   a. in front of   **b.** in back of   **c.** on top of

4. Each firefighter **is in charge of** his or her own things and must take care of them. *Be in charge of something* means:

   a. feel relaxed about it   **b.** be responsible for it   **c.** forget about it

5. Brandon wasn't interested in an office job. He likes to be **outdoors** in the fresh air. *Outdoors* means:

   a. at home   **b.** at school   **c.** outside and away from buildings

6. Brandon **applied for** a job as a firefighter. *Apply for something* means:

   a. tell people about it   **b.** ask for it (in writing)   **c.** disagree with it

7. New firefighters get their first **training** at fire school. They continue to learn on the job. *Training* means:

   a. traveling by train   **b.** trying to get a job   **c.** learning the skills for a job

8. The word *Hotshot* **refers to** a certain kind of firefighter. *Refers to* means:

   a. is about or means   **b.** comes from   **c.** is the opposite of

9. Some firefighters have to be **available** when they are needed. *Available* means:

   a. gentle   **b.** free to do something   **c.** certain

10. Firefighters work hardest during the fire **season**. *Season* means:

    a. the time of year when   **b.** a place for learning   **c.** an interview
        something happens   to do something   for a job

B These sentences use the target words and phrases **in new contexts**.
Complete them with the words and phrases in the box.

ahead of	apply for	available	ended up	is in charge of
outdoors	refers to	seasons	toward	training

1. He's the boss. He _____ everyone who works here.

2. The question "What do you do?" _____ the kind of work you do.

3. She finally made up her mind to leave the company, and she began to
_____ other jobs.

4. Doctors study for many years. They need a lot of _____.

5. Mr. Lee is busy now, but after lunch, he'll be _____ to talk to us.

6. Canada has four _____: summer, winter, spring, and fall.

7. I tried to install the new software by myself, but I _____
calling Customer Support for help.

8. We wanted to eat _____, but it was raining.

9. She is _____ him.

10. She is running _____ him.

Read each definition and look at the paragraph number in parentheses ( ). Look back at the reading to **find the target word** for each definition. Write it in the chart.

Definition	Target Word
1. a place where many trees cover a large area of land (paragraph 2)	forest
2. break or hurt something so that it cannot continue or be used (2)	
3. made of animal skin that has been prepared for use in shoes, belts, etc. (3)	
4. having a very thin part that can cut or pass through things easily (like a knife or a needle) (3)	
5. the ability to wait for a long time without becoming nervous or angry (3)	
6. things that are useful for doing a job (3)	

A firefighter may use these *tools:*

an axe

a saw

a shovel

Building on the Vocabulary

Studying Word Grammar

Remember: The parts of speech are the different kinds of words, such as nouns, verbs, and adjectives. A **verb** is a word for an action. For example, *go, fly, run,* and *play* are verbs. The words *have* and *be* are also verbs. Sometimes a word can act as a noun OR a verb. For example:

*We can't stop now. We're in a **rush**.* (noun)

*We **rushed** out the door to catch the bus.* (verb)

Are the boldfaced words below nouns or verbs? Write the abbreviation n. or v.

1. a. I like to travel by **train**. _____n._____

   b. He is going to **train** the new horse. _____

2. a. He **supports** his wife and four children. _____

   b. The president thanked the voters for their **support**. _____

3. a. I have a job **interview** on Friday. _____

   b. How many people did they **interview**? _____

4. a. The plane dropped a **bomb**. _____

   b. Will the planes **bomb** the city? _____

DEVELOPING YOUR SKILLS

Scanning

Read these questions about "Ready for Action." Scan the reading and write short answers. You do not need to write complete sentences.

1. Paragraph 2: What two words describe the work of fighting forest fires?

   _____dangerous_____ and _____

2. Who first told Brandon about jobs with the Forest Service?

   _____

3. What test did he take? _____

4. Where did he learn to fight fires? _____ and _____

5. What is a Hotshot crew? _____

Reading Between the Lines

You cannot scan the reading for quick answers to these questions. These are inference or opinion questions. To answer them, you must put information from the reading together with what you know or believe. Write complete sentences.

1. Why does the Forest Service give a test to new firefighters? _Maybe the_
   Forest Service wants to see how strong the new firefighters are, or
   maybe the test is to show the new people how hard the job is.

2. Why does Brandon say, "It's all about patience"? _____

   _____

   _____

3. Why do you think Brandon wants to join a Hotshot crew? _____

_____

_____

Discussion

Talk about these questions in a small group.

1. Fighting forest fires can be exciting. What other jobs do you think are exciting?
2. What do people in your country think of firefighters?
3. How would you feel if your husband or wife were a firefighter? Why?

Using New Words

Work with a partner. Take turns asking for and giving information. Then tell the class something about your partner.

1. When and where do you like to be **outdoors**?
2. What do you have that is made of **leather**?
3. Name two **tools** that you use to do your schoolwork.
4. Name two jobs that you would _NEVER_ **apply for**.
5. Name two things that make you lose **patience**.

Writing

Brandon learned about firefighting from people on the job. He says, "You have to trust the people with more experience." Write a paragraph about learning from other people and their experience. You can write about:

- a time when you learned something this way, or
- using your own experience to teach someone else.

CHAPTER 4

Life Is Full of Surprises

Mahmoud Arani in the classroom

GETTING READY TO READ

Talk in a small group or with the whole class.

1. Mahmoud Arani is from Iran. Do you know where Iran is or anything about its history? Tell what you know about Iran.

2. Many people leave their countries to study or to work. List some reasons why people do this.

READING

Look at the words next to the reading. Then read without stopping.

Life Is Full of Surprises

1   Mahmoud Arani is a **professor** at a small American college. He did not expect to end up in the United States, and he did not expect to teach. He grew up in Iran, and he planned to be a doctor. However, as people say, life is full of surprises.

2   Mahmoud was born in Iran near the city of Tehran. At school, he was an excellent student, the best in his class, and he was planning to study **medicine** in college. First, he had to take the university entrance exam.[1] He needed to do well to **get into** a **medical** school. Out of 50,000 high school students taking the test, only 1,000 would have the chance to study medicine in college. Mahmoud missed the **score** he needed by a few **points**. His teachers were very surprised. He took the test again. Again the news was bad. "I was **disappointed**," he remembers, "but I said, 'That is my fate.'"[2]

3   Mahmoud was also interested in languages, so he chose to study English. After college, he decided to go to the United States for an **advanced** degree[3] in this **subject**. A few months later, he entered an English as a Second Language (ESL) program. It was in Buffalo, New York, at the state university. Mahmoud was one of half a million international students who entered the United States to study that year. But he **managed to** do something that few others could. In less than two years, he went from studying ESL to teaching it at the same school!

4   On a visit home from New York, Mahmoud had an interview at a university in Tehran. They offered him a job, and he accepted it. The university made an **agreement** with him. Mahmoud said he would return to Buffalo to finish his degree, and they agreed to support him. After he finished, he would come back to teach. So Mahmoud went back to New York feeling great. He thought his future was **secure**.

5   Then something happened. There was a revolution[4] in Iran. It **caused** great changes in the country. Soon Mahmoud received a letter from his university in Tehran. It said, "We don't need any English teachers." Suddenly, his support was gone, and his future was unclear.

continued

[1] an *entrance exam* = a test someone must take to be able to enter a school

[2] *fate* = the things that will happen that a person cannot control

[3] a *degree* = what a student gets for completing a program at a college or university

[4] a *revolution* = a time of great and sudden change in a country, often by force

6   Mahmoud decided not to **give up**: He would keep working toward his degree. After much hard work, he reached his **goal**. Then, after teaching ESL in Buffalo for a while, he accepted a job at Saint Michael's College in Vermont. His students there report that he is an excellent teacher.

7   Now Mahmoud is married. He and his wife, Roya, have two children. Roya is also from Iran, and she is a doctor. Mahmoud is still interested in medicine, too. "I could go to medical school now," he says, "if I had the patience!" He does not plan to make a career change at this **stage** in his life. However, he adds, "I know that life is full of surprises. . . ."

Quick Comprehension Check

Read these sentences. Circle T (true) or F (false).

1. Mahmoud was born and grew up in Iran.   T   F

2. He wanted to study medicine and become a doctor.   T   F

3. He traveled to the United States to study medicine.   T   F

4. He expected to teach at a university in Iran.   T   F

5. The Iranian revolution happened while he was at home in Tehran.   T   F

6. The revolution changed his life.   T   F

EXPLORING VOCABULARY

Thinking about the Vocabulary

Look at the target words and phrases. Which ones are new to you? Circle them here and in the reading. Then read "Life Is Full of Surprises" again. Look at the context of each new word and phrase. Can you guess the meaning?

Target Words and Phrases			
professor (1)	**score** (2)	**subject** (3)	**caused** (5)
medicine (2)	**points** (2)	**managed to** (3)	**give up** (6)
get into (2)	**disappointed** (2)	**agreement** (4)	**goal** (6)
medical (2)	**advanced** (3)	**secure** (4)	**stage** (7)

Using the Vocabulary

Ⓐ These sentences are **about the reading**. Complete them with the words and phrases in the box.

agreement	caused	disappointed	get into	give up	goal
managed to	medicine	points	stage	subject	

1. Mahmoud wanted to study _____ so that he could become a doctor.

2. Mahmoud had to do well on a test to _____ medical school. The test decided which students could enter the school.

3. Mahmoud's test results weren't high enough. He needed a few more _____.

4. Mahmoud had to change his college plans. He couldn't do what he had hoped to do. He felt _____.

5. In college, he took many English courses. English was the _____ that he studied most.

6. Mahmoud was able to do something unusual. He _____ do something that few international students could do.

7. Mahmoud and the university made an _____. Each side made promises.

8. Great changes happened in Iran because of the revolution. The revolution _____ these changes.

9. It was hard for Mahmoud to keep going, but he didn't _____. He never stopped trying.

10. Mahmoud finally got what he wanted. He reached his _____.

11. At one time, Mahmoud wanted to become a doctor. But at this _____ of his life, he is happy as a professor.

Ⓑ These sentences use the target words and phrases **in new contexts**. Complete them with the words and phrases in the box.

agreement	caused	disappointed	gave up	get into	goal
managed to	medicine	points	stages	subjects	

1. Two companies made an _____ to develop software together.

2. Children go through different _____ as they grow.

3. College students can take courses in math, history, education, and many other _____.

4. There was an accident on the road ahead of us. It _____ traffic problems.

5. I kept calling, but your phone was always busy, so finally I _____.

6. You need good grades if you want to _____ a good college.

7. I couldn't open the door, but I _____ get in through a window.

8. Doctors, dentists, and nurses all work in the field of _____.

9. I was _____ when my team didn't win.

10. Jack's main _____ in life is to make a lot of money.

11. In basketball, a player usually gets two _____ for getting the ball in the basket.

C Read these sentences. Write the **boldfaced** target words next to their definitions.

a. I didn't get a good **score** on the test, so I was disappointed.

b. The **professor** is available to talk with students during her office hours.

c. He can relax and stop worrying about money. He has a **secure** job now.

d. You can get good **medical** care at that hospital.

e. We are both studying Spanish, but I'm a beginner and he's in an **advanced** class.

Target Words   **Definitions**

1. ____*professor*____ = a teacher at a college or university

2. _____ = not expected to change or be in any danger

3. _____ = relating to a school subject at a difficult level

4. _____ = relating to medicine and the care of people who are sick or hurt

5. _____ = the number of points someone gets on a test or in a game

Building on the Vocabulary

Studying Word Grammar

Give up is a **phrasal verb.** Phrasal verbs have two parts: a verb (such as *give, get, turn*) and a particle (such as *up, out, off*). The meaning of the phrasal verb is different from the meaning of the verb alone.

A In Unit 1, you learned the phrasal verbs *come up, give up, end up,* and *get into.* Use them to complete these sentences.

1. He couldn't _____ the class; it was already full.

2. The team was losing, but they didn't _____.

3. I try to get to bed early, but I often _____ watching a late movie.

4. Call me if any problems _____.

B On a piece of paper, write three sentences with the phrasal verbs in Part A.

Example: My friend got into college when he was only 16.

DEVELOPING YOUR SKILLS

Reading for Details

Read these sentences. Then scan "Life Is Full of Surprises" for the answers. If the reading doesn't give the information, check (✓) *It doesn't say.*

	True	False	It doesn't say.
1. Mahmoud was born in Iran.	✓		
2. He studied English in college.			
3. He went to the United States to look for a job.			
4. Mahmoud's visit to Iran lasted for six months.			
5. The revolution in Iran happened while he was there.			
6. He received a degree from the state university in Buffalo, New York.			
7. He is a husband and a father.			
8. He and his wife are both professors.			
9. He is now planning to enter medical school.			
10. All of Mahmoud's family is in the United States.			

Understanding Cause and Effect

Sentences with *because* explain why something happens. Complete the
following sentences using information from "Life Is Full of Surprises."

1. Mahmoud's grade on the exam surprised his teachers because <u>he was</u>
   <u>the best student in his class, but his score wasn't high enough for</u>
   <u>medical school.</u>

2. Mahmoud decided to study English because _____
   _____.

3. He went to the United States because _____
   _____.

4. As an international student, Mahmoud was unusual because _____
   _____.

5. He lost the chance to teach in Tehran because _____
   _____.

6. He doesn't plan to start medical school now because _____
   _____.

Discussion

Talk with your class about these questions.

1. How many people in the class agree that "life is full of surprises"? Are
   surprises a good thing in life? Why or why not?

2. How many people in the class would like to teach English? What are some
   reasons why people in the class do and do not want to?

3. How did your teacher become a teacher of English?

Using New Words

**Work with a partner. Choose five target words or phrases from the list on
page 28. On a piece of paper, use each word or phrase in a sentence.**

Writing

Choose a topic. Write a paragraph.

1. Describe a time in your life when you set a goal and didn't give up. What
   were you trying to do? What made it hard? How did you reach your goal?

2. Think back to an earlier stage in your life. Write about a time when you
   wanted something very much. Did you get what you wanted, or were you
   disappointed? Explain.

Wrap-up

REVIEWING VOCABULARY

 Match these nouns with their definitions. There are two extra words.

agreement	detail	goal	hardware	~~insect~~
interview	report	skill	software	subject

1. _____insect_____ = a very small animal (such as a fly) that has six legs

2. _____ = something you want to do in the future

3. _____ = a promise made between two people or groups

4. _____ = a meeting to ask someone questions

5. _____ = one fact or small piece of information

6. _____ = a group of instructions that tell a computer what to do

7. _____ = a topic or an area that you study in school

8. _____ = an ability to do something, especially because you
have learned it

B **Complete these sentences. There are two extra words or phrases.**

by accident	came up	exactly	fear
in charge of	leather	make up her mind	manage to
pay attention	refer to		

1. He should turn off the TV and _____ to his homework!

2. She has two job offers. Now she has to _____.

3. A problem _____, so I needed some advice.

4. The computer isn't working, but I'm sure Yoko will _____ fix it.

5. I took your book _____. Sorry, I thought it was mine.

6. The words *they* and *them* can _____ people or things.

7. I don't know the time _____, but it's about 10:00.

8. Who is _____ training the new workers?

EXPANDING VOCABULARY

 Remember: The parts of speech are the different kinds of words, such as nouns, verbs, and adjectives. An **adjective** is a word that describes a noun. Adjectives can come before nouns: *a nice person, a great idea.* They can also come after the verb *be* and linking verbs such as *feel, look,* and *sound: She wasn't nice to me. Your idea sounds great.*

There are one or two adjectives in each sentence. Circle the adjectives.

1. That knife is (new) and very (sharp.)
2. They looked calm and relaxed before the game.
3. He is available to meet with us at 4:00.
4. I was disappointed when I heard the final score.
5. The boss is interested in getting better software.
6. Certain kinds of birds cannot fly.
7. I worry that Ann's job is not secure.
8. She told the boys to be gentle with the little cat.

B Many words belong to **word families**. When you learn a new word, it is a good idea to learn other words in the same family.

Use words from each family in the chart to complete the sentence.

	Nouns	Verbs	Adjectives
1.	application	apply	
2.	communication	communicate	
3.	trainer training	train	trained

1. Before you can get an interview for the job, you must complete an
   _____.
2. People in business all over the world _____ in English.
3. **a.** Medical schools _____ doctors.
   b. His army career began with six months of basic _____.
   c. The hotel workers all seemed well-_____.

PLAYING WITH WORDS

Complete the sentences with words you studied in Chapters 1–4. Write the words in the puzzle.

Across

1. Most plural nouns in English end in -s, but **certain**_____ ones don't.

4. I closed my eyes and tried to **i**_____ being on a beach.

6. My shoes are made of **l**_____.

7. We expected him; **h**_____, he didn't come.

9. Forest fires **d**_____ trees.

11. I saw her coming **t**_____ me across the room.

12. Teachers and parents need a lot of **p**_____.

13. She had a long **c**_____ as a banker.

Down

2. These shoes are **a**_____ in four different colors.

3. They **d**_____ software for businesses.

5. She was standing **a**_____ of me in line.

8. We're developing a plan, but it's still at an early **s**_____.

10. They work hard to **s**_____ their families.

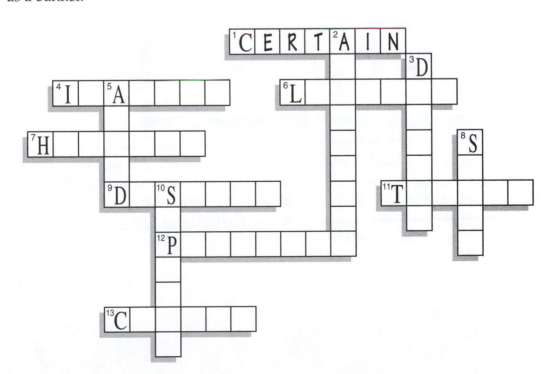

BUILDING DICTIONARY SKILLS

Finding Words in the Dictionary, Part 1

Ⓐ **Guidewords** help you find words in the dictionary. Look at pages 114 and 115 below. The guidewords are *cater* and *center*. *Cater* is the first word on the left page; *center* is the last word on the right page.

cater	114

ca·ter /ˈkeɪtɚ/ *v* [I,T] to provide and serve food and drinks at a party: *Who's catering your daughter's wedding?* —**caterer** *n*
 cater to sb *phr v* [T] to provide a particular group of people with something that they need or want: *newspapers that cater to business…*

115	center

cell /sɛl/ *n* **1** a small room in a police station or prison where prisoners are kept **2** the smallest part of an animal or plant that can exist on its own: *red blood cells*
cel·lar /ˈsɛlɚ/ *n* a room under a house or restaurant: *a wine cellar*
cel·list /ˈtʃɛlɪst/ *n* someone

Will these words be on pages 114–115? Check (✓) *Yes* or *No*.

	Yes	No
1. certain		
2. cause		
3. calm		
4. cent		
5. CD-ROM		
6. central		

Ⓑ A **compound word** is made up of two words. Some compound words are written as one word (*birthday, homework*); others are written as two words (*ice cream, good night*); and others are written with a hyphen (*good-looking, bird-brained*). The *Longman Dictionary of American English* treats these words as one word and lists them with other words in alphabetical order, for example:
good
good-bye
good evening
goodness

Write the following words in the order you would find them in the dictionary. (Note: In the examples below, the small numbers¹ and² after a word are superscripts. The dictionary entry for *outline*¹ gives the meanings of the noun *outline;* the entry for *outline*² gives the meanings of the verb *outline.*)

outer space	out¹	outdoors	outdoor
outline¹	outline²	out-of-state	outlive

1. _____*out*¹_____   4. _____   7. _____

2. _____   5. _____   8. _____

3. _____   6. _____

 Phrasal verbs do not have their own entries in *The Longman Dictionary of American English.* They are part of the entry for the verb.

Look at this entry for the verb *end.* Circle the two phrasal verbs.

---

end² *v* [I,T] to finish or stop, or to make something do this: *World War II ended in 1945.* | *Janet's party didn't end until 4 o'clock in the morning.* | *Lucy decided to end her relationship with Jeff.*
  end in sth *phr v* [T] to have a particular result or to finish in a particular way: *The meeting **ended in** a huge argument.*
  end up *phr v* [I] to come to be in a place, situation, or condition that you did not expect or intend: *Whenever we go out to dinner I always **end up** paying the bill.*

IT'S ALL IN YOUR HEAD

CHAPTER 5

Food for Thought

Morning coffee

GETTING READY TO READ

Talk in a small group or with the whole class.

1. How many people in the group drink:

   _____ coffee

   _____ tea

   _____ soda such as Coke or Pepsi

   _____ chocolate drinks

2. All the drinks in the list have caffeine.[1] Do you know any other drinks with caffeine?

3. When and why do people like drinks with caffeine?

[1] *caffeine* = a substance (in coffee, tea, and some other drinks) that helps tired minds wake up

READING

Look at the words and pictures next to the reading. Then read without stopping. Don't worry about new words. Don't stop to use a dictionary. Just keep reading!

Food for Thought

1   The foods you eat **supply** your body with energy. Your body needs energy to move and even to sleep. One part of your body uses a surprising **amount** of energy. This body part is small—only 2–3% of your total **weight**—but it uses 20–30% of the energy from your food. Can you guess what it is? It is your brain.

2   You already know that drugs **affect** the brain. Did you know that food affects it, too? Different types of food affect the brain in different ways. Sometimes we can feel the changes that food makes in our brains. For example, most people can feel an **immediate** change after drinking coffee. It is the caffeine in coffee that affects the brain. Caffeine usually makes people feel more **awake**. After a cup of coffee, a person can think and make decisions more quickly.

3   Other foods affect the brain in ways that we cannot see or feel. We don't **realize** how they influence us. However, everything we eat matters. Our food affects how **smart** we are and how well we remember things. It also affects how long we can concentrate.[1] For example, scientists know that:

1. Eating breakfast makes students do better on tests.

2. Spinach,[2] berries,[3] and other colorful fruits and vegetables help keep older brains from slowing down.

3. Eating large amounts of animal fat (in meat and cheese, for example) makes learning more difficult.

4. Fish really is "brain food." For years, many people believed that eating fish was good for the brain. Now scientists are finding that this is true.

4   For millions of years, the brains of early human beings[4] stayed the same size. They weighed only about one pound (400–500 grams). Then, during the last million years or so,

continued

[1] *concentrate* = think carefully

[2] *spinach* = a dark green, leafy vegetable

[3] *berries*

[4] *early human beings* = the first people who lived

there was a big **increase** in brain size. The human brain grew to about three pounds. This increase in brain size **meant** an increase in brain power. With bigger, stronger brains, human beings became smart enough to build boats and **invent** written languages. They developed forms of music and **created** works of art.[5] Some scientists say that these changes happened after people started to eat seafood.[6] Seafood **contains** a certain kind of fat, omega-3 fat. **According to** these scientists, omega-3 fat caused the increase in brain size. Today, brain scientists agree: This fat is still important for healthy brains. They also say that most of us are not getting enough of it.

[5] *works of art* = the things that artists make

[6] *seafood*

5   Did you know that the brains of adults continue to grow and change? The foods you eat affect how your brain grows. They affect how well you learn and remember things. Maybe you never thought about that before. **Luckily**, it is never too late to start **feeding** your brain well!

Quick Comprehension Check

Read these sentences. Circle T (true) or F (false).

1. Your brain is small, but it uses a lot of energy.   T   F

2. The foods you eat affect the way your brain works.   T   F

3. When a food causes changes in your brain, you can always   T   F
    feel it.

4. Maybe eating fish helped make the human brain bigger.   T   F

5. All kinds of fat are bad for your brain.   T   F

6. Children's brains grow and change, but adult brains don't.   T   F

EXPLORING VOCABULARY

Thinking about the Vocabulary

Look at the target words and phrases. Which ones are new to you? Circle them here and in the reading. Then read "Food for Thought" again. Look at the context of each new word and phrase. Can you guess the meaning?

Target Words and Phrases			
supply (1)	**immediate** (2)	**increase** (4)	**contains** (4)
amount (1)	**awake** (2)	**meant** (4)	**according to** (4)
weight (1)	**realize** (3)	**invent** (4)	**luckily** (5)
affect (2)	**smart** (3)	**created** (4)	**feeding** (5)

Using the Vocabulary

 Complete the sentences. Write: *amount, awake, feeding,* and *increase.*

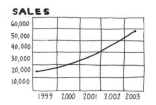

1. She's _____; he's not.

2. There was an _____ in sales.

3. He's _____ the baby.

4. Write the _____ on the check.

B These sentences are **about the reading**. Complete them with the words and phrases in the box.

according to	affects	contains	create	immediate	invented
luckily	meant	realize	smart	supply	weight

1. Food gives us energy. When we eat, we _____ our bodies with energy.

2. Your brain is not very heavy. It is only 2–3% of your total body _____.

3. Drugs influence, or cause changes in, the brain. Food _____ it, too.

4. Sometimes a drug or food affects the brain quickly and people feel the difference very soon. They feel an _____ change.

5. Many people know about coffee, but they don't _____ that other foods affect them, too.

6. The right food can make a person more intelligent. Our food influences how _____ we are.

7. An increase in the size of the human brain _____ more brain power. The increase led to that result.

8. People developed spoken languages first. Later, they _____ writing. People needed larger brains to think of this idea.

9. Early humans also began to produce music and art. They started to _____ these things.

10. Some scientists say that eating seafood caused big changes. _____ these scientists, seafood helped the human brain to grow.

11. There is omega-3 fat in seafood. Seafood _____ this kind of fat.

12. Maybe you never thought about eating "brain food" before. _____, it's not too late. You can start now, and that is a good thing.

These sentences use the target words and phrases **in new contexts**. Complete them with the words and phrases in the box.

according to	affects	contain	create	immediate	invents
luckily	meant	realize	smart	supplies	weight

1. There was a car accident there today. _____, no one was hurt.

2. She's a _____ girl, and she does very well in school.

3. Fruit is often sold by _____—$1.00 a pound, for example.

4. There were no surprises in the report. It didn't _____ any new information.

5. The weather often _____ people's travel plans.

6. He needed _____ medical care, so we rushed him to the hospital.

7. She was already in bed when I called. I didn't _____ it was so late.

8. The company _____ its workers with all the tools they need.

9. We got a foot of snow, so that _____ we had no school the next day.

10. I have no more patience with them. They just _____ problems for everyone else.

11. When someone _____ a new machine, product, or way of doing something, we call that person an inventor.

12. _____ the newspaper, there will be a lot of jobs in that field in the years ahead.

Building on the Vocabulary

Studying Collocations

Remember: Collocations are words that go together. Certain adjectives go with the noun *amount.*

- Use *large* + *amount* but not "*big amount.*"
- Use *small* + *amount* but not "*little amount.*"

Use *amount* + *of* + a noncount noun (such as *energy, time, money,* or *work*).

Example: *I never carry large amounts of money.*

Write three sentences with *amount of*.

1. _____

   _____

2. _____

   _____

3. _____

   _____

DEVELOPING YOUR SKILLS

Scanning

Read these statements about "Food for Thought." Scan the reading for the information you need to complete them. Answers inside quotation marks (" ") must match the words in the reading exactly.

1. The foods you eat give your body _____.

2. The brain makes up only _____% of your body's total weight.

3. The brain uses _____% of the energy from your food.

4. The _____ in coffee makes people feel more awake.

5. Scientists know that:

   a. "Eating breakfast_____."

   b. "_____" are good for older brains.

   c. "Eating large amounts of animal fat _____ _____."

   d. "_____ really is 'brain food.' "

6. Early human brains grew from about _____ to about _____.

7. With bigger, stronger brains, human beings were able to build _____, invent _____, and create _____.

Thinking about the Main Idea

Complete the main idea of "Food for Thought."

The foods you eat affect how _____.

Discussion

Talk about these questions with a partner.

1. At what times during the day do you think your brain works best? Why?

2. How much would you change the way you eat to make yourself smarter? What is one thing you would do? What is one thing you would not do?

3. What questions would you like to ask scientists about food and the brain? Make a list.

Using New Words

Work with a partner. Take turns completing each statement. Use one of the words or phrases in parentheses.

1. I'm (glad/sorry) that somebody **invented** . . .

2. I'm (usually/rarely) **awake** . . .

3. **Luckily**, (I/my family) . . .

4. **According to** my (parents/friends), . . .

5. (People/Children) often don't **realize** that . . .

Writing

Write a paragraph about something you like to eat or drink. When do you usually have it? How does it affect you? Do you think it's good or bad for you? Why?

CHAPTER 6

Your Memory at Work

Trying to remember . . .

GETTING READY TO READ

Talk with a partner or in a small group.

1. Look at the things in the list. Which ones are usually easy for you to remember? Which ones are hard?

people's names	colors	words to songs
people's faces	music	information from classes
numbers	new vocabulary in English	other: _____

2. When you MUST remember something, what do you do? How do you help yourself remember it?

READING

Look at the words and picture next to the reading. Then read without stopping.

Your Memory at Work

1   You have two basic types of memory: short-**term** memory and long-term memory. Things you see or hear first enter your short-term memory. Very little of this information passes on into your long-term memory. Does this mean you have a bad memory? Not at all.[1]

2   Your short-term memory has a certain job. Its job is to **store** information for a few seconds only. Your short-term memory is at work when you **look up** a phone number, call the number, and then forget it. You remembered the number just long enough to use it. Then it **disappeared** from your memory. That's really a good thing. Imagine if your memory held every number, every face, and every word you ever knew!

3   However, some information is important to remember for a longer time. Then it must pass from short-term to long-term memory. Sometimes we tell ourselves to remember something. We might also **practice** it: "OK, don't forget: 555-1212, 555-1212." Usually, we don't even think about it. Our brain makes the decision for us. It decides to store the information or let it go.

4   The brain seems to make the decision by asking two questions:

    1. Does the information affect our **emotions**? **That is,** does it make us happy, sad, excited, or **upset**?

    2. Does the information **concern** something we already know, so our brain can store it with something already there?

An answer of "Yes" means that the new information enters long-term memory. That means the brain creates new **connections** among brain cells.[2] These connections form in a **region** of the brain called the *cerebral cortex*.[3] It is the largest part of the brain.

5   After a piece of information enters your long-term memory, how do you get it back? Sometimes your brain may seem like a **deep,** dark **closet.** You open the door to look for

continued

[1] *not at all* = in no way

[2] a *cell* = in any living thing, the smallest part that can live by itself

[3] the *cerebral cortex*

something—you are sure it is in there somewhere—but you cannot find it. Maybe the information really is **not** there **anymore.** Information disappears when connections among brain cells become **weak.** They get weak if time passes and the connections are not used. That is why it is good to read your lecture[4] **notes** soon after the class. Don't wait too long to "look in the closet."

[4] a *lecture* = a long talk about a subject to a group or class

6   To keep the memory of something strong, think of it often. For example, look at those lecture notes the next day. Look at them the day after that, too. Every time you think about something, the connections in the brain get stronger. Then it is easier to remember the information when you need it.

Quick Comprehension Check

Read these sentences. Circle T (true) or F (false).

1. People have two types of memory.   T   F

2. Your short-term memory holds information for only a   T   F
    few days.

3. All information should go to your long-term memory.   T   F

4. We usually remember information that affects how we feel.   T   F

5. Information in long-term memory will always be there.   T   F

6. There are things you can do to help yourself remember   T   F
    information.

Exploring Vocabulary

Thinking about the Vocabulary

Look at the target words and phrases. Which ones are new to you? Circle them here and in the reading. Then read "Your Memory at Work" again. Look at the context of each new word and phrase. Can you guess the meaning?

Target Words and Phrases			
term (1)	**practice** (3)	**concern** (4)	**closet** (5)
store (2)	**emotions** (4)	**connections** (4)	**not . . . anymore** (5)
look up (2)	**that is** (4)	**region** (4)	**weak** (5)
disappeared (2)	**upset** (4)	**deep** (5)	**notes** (5)

Using the Vocabulary

 These sentences are about the reading. What is the meaning of each boldfaced word? Circle a, b, or c.

1. Information first enters your short-**term** memory. *Term* means:

    a. training **b.** an amount of time **c.** movement

2. Your short-term memory can **store** information for a short time only. *Store* means:

    a. cause **b.** keep **c.** sell

3. When you need a phone number, you can **look up** the number in the phone book. *Look up* means:

    a. come up **b.** get into **c.** try to find (information)

4. Some information leaves your brain quickly. It **disappears**. *Disappears* means:

    a. goes away completely **b.** moves ahead **c.** communicates

5. It is easier to remember new facts or ideas when they **concern** something we already know. *Concern* means:

    a. be about **b.** destroy **c.** end up

6. New **connections** form among brain cells when we learn something new. *Connections* means places:

    a. where nothing happens **b.** where things come together **c.** where something stops

7. The cerebral cortex is a **region** of the brain. *Region* means:

    a. a tool **b.** a season **c.** an area

8. Sometimes a fact was in someone's brain, but it's **not** there **anymore**. *Not . . . anymore* means:

    a. not . . . now **b.** not . . . exactly **c.** not . . . luckily

9. We forget things when connections among brain cells get **weak**. *Weak* means:

    a. sharp **b.** not strong **c.** secure

10. Students usually study their **notes** from class before they take a test. *Notes* means:

    a. information in writing **b.** things to eat **c.** professors

B These sentences use the target words and phrases **in new contexts**.
Complete them with the words and phrases in the box.

concerns	connection	disappeared	looked up	not anymore
region	store	take notes	terms	weak

1. Students often _____ in class about things they want to remember.

2. I _____ the word *connection* in my dictionary.

3. We watched the plane until it _____ into the clouds.

4. He lives in a _____ where they get a lot of snow.

5. Where do you _____ your summer clothes during the winter?

6. At his university, there are two _____ in the school year: fall semester and spring semester.

7. I just received this letter from the bank. It _____ my credit card.

8. She gave up coffee. She used to drink ten cups a day, but _____.

9. Being sick for so long made him lose weight and feel _____.

10. When one fact, idea, or event affects another, we can say there is a _____ between them.

 C Read each definition and look at the paragraph number in parentheses ( ).
Look back at the reading to **find the target word or phrase** for each
definition. Write it in the chart.

Definition	Target Word or Phrase
1. do something again and again to develop a skill (3)	
2. strong feelings such as love or hate (4)	
3. (a phrase meaning) "What I mean to say is . . ." (4)	
4. unhappy or worried (4)	
5. going far in or far down (5)	
6. a very small room where people usually hang clothes or store things (5)	

Building on the Vocabulary

> ### Studying Word Grammar
>
> Remember: The parts of speech are the different kinds of words, such as nouns, verbs, adjectives, and **adverbs**. An adverb can describe:
>
> - a verb: *She **gently** <u>touched</u> my hand. Please <u>go</u> **ahead**.*
> - an adjective: *I felt **very** <u>relaxed</u>. Is it <u>sharp</u> **enough**?*
> - a whole statement: ***Luckily,** <u>it didn't rain much</u>.*

Circle the adverbs that describe the underlined words.

1. I (quickly) <u>realized</u> that it was a mistake.
2. Please be sure the door is securely <u>closed</u>.
3. She <u>spoke</u> calmly, but I knew she was upset.
4. He's a very <u>smart</u> boy.
5. By accident, <u>I took the wrong bus</u>.
6. We need to <u>leave</u> immediately.
7. The map <u>shows</u> exactly where to go.
8. The runner was too <u>weak</u> to continue.

DEVELOPING YOUR SKILLS

Understanding Topics of Paragraphs

A **Where is the information about these topics in "Your Memory at Work"? Skim the reading and write the paragraph number.**

____4____ **a.** How the brain deals with new information

_____ **b.** Types of memory

_____ **c.** Trouble remembering information

_____ **d.** Keeping connections among brain cells strong

_____ **e.** What short-term memory does

_____ **f.** Ways to pass information from short-term to long-term memory

B Write a sentence or two about each topic in Part A, beginning with the topic of the first paragraph and continuing in order. Use information from the reading, but do not copy sentences. Use your own words.

1. The two basic types of memory are short-term and long-term memory.
    _____
    _____

2. _____
    _____
    _____

3. _____
    _____
    _____

4. _____
    _____
    _____

5. _____
    _____
    _____

6. _____
    _____
    _____

Summarizing

Complete the summary of "Your Memory at Work." Write one or more words on each line.

The two basic types of memory are short-term memory and
_____(1)_____

_____(2)_____. Information stays in short-term memory for

_____(3)_____. Then the information often _____(4)_____.

When information is important to remember, it has to pass to

_____(5)_____. When information enters long-term memory,

_____(6)_____ are formed among brain cells. You make them stronger

each time you _____(7)_____ the information.

Discussion

Talk about these questions in a small group.

1. What helps you remember new words in English?
2. How do you study vocabulary for a test?
3. What kinds of words are easy to remember? What kinds of words are hard?

Using New Words

Work with a partner. Choose five target words or phrases from the list on page 49. On a piece of paper, use each word or phrase in a sentence.

Writing

Choose a Discussion question above and write a paragraph about it. You can begin with:

- *Several things help me remember new words in English.*
- *I have several ways to study vocabulary for a test.*
- *Certain kinds of words are easier to remember than others.*

CHAPTER 7

Sleep and the Brain

Deep in Stage 4

GETTING READY TO READ

Talk with a partner or in a small group.

1. How many hours of sleep do you usually get?
2. Would you like to sleep more? Less? Explain why.
3. Do you think these statements are true or false?

    a. Our brains are completely at rest (they "turn off")   T   F
       when we sleep.

    b. We spend only 2–4% of our sleep time dreaming.   T   F

    c. When we are dreaming, we are most completely   T   F
       asleep. It is hardest to wake us up then.

Look for the answers to 3. a–c in the reading.

READING

Look at the words and picture next to the reading. Then read without stopping.

Sleep and the Brain

1   Human beings, like all mammals,[1] need sleep. People need an **average** of 7.5 hours a night. However, the average amount may not be right for you, just as the average-size shoe might not be right for your foot.

2   People may not need the same amount of sleep, but everyone needs the same two types of sleep. Your sleep is **divided** between REM sleep (*REM* is **pronounced** "rem") and NREM sleep (pronounced "en-rem" or "non-rem"):

- *REM* comes from the words "rapid[2] eye movement." During this type of sleep, your eyes move quickly. This movement shows that you are dreaming.

- *NREM* means "non-REM," or no eye movement. This is dreamless sleep, and it has four stages.

3   During the night, you go through several sleep cycles. A cycle is a **set**, or group, of events. Events in cycles happen again and again, like the cycle of seasons that happens every year. In each sleep cycle, you go from a light sleep to a deeper sleep and back again. You enter your first cycle when you fall asleep, and it lasts about 90 minutes. This cycle **includes** both REM sleep and the four stages of NREM sleep. It usually goes like this:

1. You begin with a **period** of light NREM sleep. This type of sleep is called Stage 1 sleep. During Stage 1 sleep, a noise could easily wake you up. This first period of Stage 1 sleep lasts less than 15 minutes.

2. Next, you move into another kind of NREM sleep for about 15–20 minutes. It is not so easy to wake you up from this type of sleep. It is called Stage 2 sleep. During the night, you spend about half your sleep time in Stage 2.

3. A short period of Stage 3 sleep is next. This marks the beginning of deep sleep. Your brain becomes less

[1] *mammals* = animals that get milk from their mothers when young

[2] *rapid* = fast

continued

active, and you breathe more slowly. Your muscles[3] relax.

4. Stage 4 follows Stage 3 and lasts 20 to 30 minutes. These two stages are a lot **alike**, but Stage 4 is your deepest sleep. Adults usually get all their Stage 4 sleep during the first few hours of the night. During this stage, some people talk or walk in their sleep.

5. Next, you return to the level of Stage 2 sleep for a short time. Your heart **rate** and your breathing get faster.

6. Then you enter REM sleep. Your brain becomes very active for 10 to 20 minutes, and you have dreams. Your body doesn't move, except for your eyes. **In fact**, your body seems to be paralyzed during REM sleep. That is, it seems unable to move.

7. You return to Stage 2 sleep. This marks the end of your first sleep cycle of the night.

[3] *muscles*

4   In most cases, you will go through a **series** of four to six sleep cycles each night. During the night, the cycles change. The amount of deep sleep **decreases**. You start to spend more time dreaming. **In general**, you spend about 20% of the night in REM sleep.

5   Why do people need sleep? Is it more for our bodies or for our brains? No one really knows. However, it is clear that sleep is important. What happens if people don't get enough? **Research** shows that we forget words, we are less **creative**, and we react[4] more slowly. You can probably think of other **effects** of not getting enough sleep. We all know we need it. Maybe future research will tell us why.

[4] *react* = feel or do something because of something that just happened

Quick Comprehension Check

Read these sentences. Circle T (true) or F (false).

1. All adults need the same amount of sleep each night.   T   F

2. We experience two basic types of sleep.   T   F

3. Your eyes move when you dream.   T   F

4. REM sleep is deep and dreamless.   T   F

5. During NREM sleep, we go through several stages.   T   F

6. Scientists still can't explain why we need sleep.   T   F

EXPLORING VOCABULARY

Thinking about the Vocabulary

Look at the target words and phrases. Which ones are new to you? Circle them here and in the reading. Then read "Sleep and the Brain" again. Look at the context of each new word and phrase. Can you guess the meaning?

Target Words and Phrases

average (1)	includes (3)	rate (3)	in general (4)
divided (2)	period (3)	in fact (3)	research (5)
pronounced (2)	active (3)	series (4)	creative (5)
set (3)	alike (3)	decreases (4)	effects (5)

Using the Vocabulary

A These sentences are **about the reading**. Complete them with the words in the box.

active	average	creative	decreases	divided	effects
includes	rate	research	series	set	

1. People need an _____ of 7.5 hours of sleep. This is the usual amount, but some people need more and others need less.

2. Our sleep is _____ between two types of sleep. We spend part of the night in REM sleep and part in NREM sleep.

3. A _____ is a group of things that belong together or a group of events that have a connection, like the different types of sleep in a sleep cycle.

4. REM sleep and NREM sleep are both part of your first sleep cycle. This cycle _____ both types of sleep.

5. During Stages 3 and 4, your brain is less _____ than usual. Your brain doesn't do so much.

6. Your heart _____ tells how fast your heart is working (for example, 60 or 70 times a minute).

7. During the night, you go through a _____ of four to six sleep cycles. This means the cycles happen one after another, in order: the first cycle, then the second, the third, and so on.

8. During the night, the type of sleep you get changes. Your dream time increases and your deep sleep time _____.

9. Scientists do _____ on sleep. They study it to learn new things about it.

10. When we don't get enough sleep, it is harder to think of new ideas or different ways to do things. We are less _____.

11. Forgetting words, thinking more slowly, getting angry more easily—these are some of the _____, or results, of not getting enough sleep.

B These sentences use the target words **in new contexts. Complete them with the words in the box.**

active	average	creative	decrease	divided	effect
included	rates	research	series	sets	

1. One hundred _____ by two is fifty.

2. Some animals sleep during the day and are _____ at night.

3. They own two _____ of dishes, one for everyday use and one for special meals.

4. *Superman—The Movie* was the first in a long _____ of Superman movies.

5. Artists are _____ people. They are always thinking of new ideas.

6. This is a very smart class. Everyone's grades are far above the _____.

7. Marie and Bill plan to save more money, so they will _____ their spending.

8. All her English practice had a great _____ on her skills.

9. These scientists do _____ on the brain and how different foods affect it.

10. Children learn at different _____. Some learn quickly, others more slowly.

11. My class _____ students from South America. Two of my classmates were Colombian.

Read these sentences. Write the boldfaced words or phrases next to their definitions.

a. How do you **pronounce** your last name?

b. Each **period** at the high school is 50 minutes long.

c. She and her sister look **alike**, but they are very different.

d. **In general**, I take good notes, but sometimes I don't understand them later!

e. Their school term is almost over. **In fact**, Friday is the last day of classes.

Target Words/Phrases   Definitions

1. _____ = almost exactly the same

2. _____ = an amount of time

3. _____ = usually, in most cases

4. _____ = say the sound of a letter or word the correct way

5. _____ = This is a phrase used to add more information, often surprising information.

Building on the Vocabulary

> ### Studying Word Grammar
>
> The verb *affect* and the noun *effect* are different.
>
> - Use *affect* to mean "make changes in": *Will missing class **affect** my grade?*
> - Use *effect* to refer to a result: *All that candy had a bad **effect** on her teeth.*

A **Complete the sentences with *affects* or *effects*.**

1. The weather often _____ my plans for the weekend.

2. I'm feeling the _____ of too little sleep.

3. A cold usually _____ your ability to smell things.

4. The new drug is not yet for sale. Researchers are still studying its

   _____.

B **Write your own sentences with *affect* and *effect*.**

1. _____

2. _____

DEVELOPING YOUR SKILLS

Reading for Details

Read these sentences. Then reread "Sleep and the Brain" for the answers. If the reading doesn't give the information, check (✓) *It doesn't say.*

	True	False	It doesn't say.
1. The average person needs 7.5 hours of sleep a night.			
2. The two basic types of sleep are REM and NREM sleep.			
3. People's eyes move quickly during NREM sleep.			
4. Most people never remember any dreams.			
5. Stage 1 sleep is very light.			
6. People spend about half the night in Stage 2 sleep.			
7. People start dreaming during Stage 3 sleep.			
8. Some people walk in their sleep while they dream.			
9. About 20% of people talk in their sleep.			
10. Too little sleep has bad effects on people.			

Summarizing

Complete this summary of "Sleep and the Brain." Write one or more words on each line.

People need different amounts of _____, but everyone

needs the same _____: REM and NREM sleep. During NREM
                         (2)

sleep, we go through four _____, from light sleep to deep sleep.
                                (3)

We dream during _____ and our _____ move
                        (4)   (5)

quickly. Researchers know _____, but they don't know
                                   (6)

_____.
        (7)

Interviewing

How sleepy are you? Work with a partner, and take turns asking the questions below.* Write your partner's answers. Use numbers:

0 = No   1 = Probably not   2 = Maybe   3 = Probably

WOULD YOU FALL ASLEEP WHILE YOU WERE . . .	
1. sitting and reading?	
2. watching TV?	
3. riding in a car for an hour?	
4. lying down in the afternoon?	
5. sitting and talking to someone?	
6. sitting quietly after lunch?	
7. sitting in a car that is stopped in traffic for a few minutes?	
Total:	

Add up the numbers, and tell your partner the total.

0–6: That's great! You're getting enough sleep.

7–8: You're average.

9 and up: Get more sleep!

*Based on the Epworth Sleepiness Scale designed by Murray W. Johns, M.D.

Using New Words

Ask and answer these questions with a partner. Use one of the words or phrases in parentheses. Then tell the class something about your partner.

1. What is the **average** number of hours you (sleep/spend on homework) a night?
2. How much is 100 **divided** by (10/25)?
3. **In general**, do you like (sweet/salty) foods?
4. Do you and anyone in your family (look/think) **alike**?
5. What is a good job for someone who is very (**creative/active**)?

Writing

Are you a light sleeper (everything wakes you up) or a heavy sleeper (nothing wakes you up)? Do you get enough sleep in general? What happens when you don't get enough? Write a paragraph about yourself as a sleeper.

CHAPTER 8

In Your Dreams

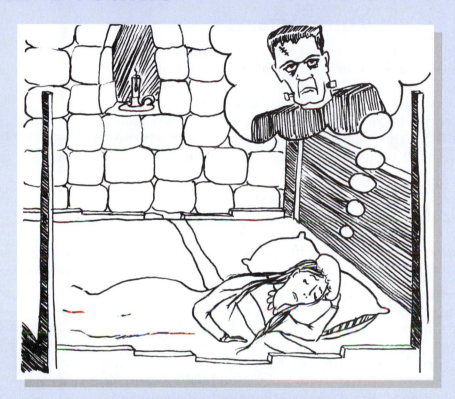

The idea for the story of Frankenstein came to writer Mary Shelley in a dream.

GETTING READY TO READ

Talk in a small group or with the whole class.

1. What's happening in the picture above?
2. How often do you remember your dreams?
3. What do you remember about your dreams?
4. Do you think people can get creative ideas while they're sleeping?
5. Do you think people can find the answers to problems in their sleep?
6. Do you think animals dream?

READING

Look at the words and pictures next to the reading. Then read without stopping.

In Your Dreams

1   Bruno Beckham has a good job. He also has a new job offer. He has to make a decision **right away**, but he isn't sure **whether or not** he should accept the offer. What will he do? He's not going to make up his mind tonight. "I'll know in the morning," he says. Why? Will the right answer come to Bruno in his dreams? "I don't know," he says, "but **whenever** I have a big decision to make, I have to sleep on it."

2   When you face a big decision, do your friends say, "Sleep on it!"? People in Italy say, "Dormici su." It means exactly the same thing. In France, they say, "La nuit porte conseil." This means "The night brings advice." People in many **cultures** believe that something **useful** happens during sleep. But what happens, and why?

3   Maybe the answer can be found in our dreams. Many people believe that dreams help us in our **daily** lives. The famous German composer[1] Beethoven believed this. He said that he wrote music that came to him in dreams. The American boxer[2] Floyd Patterson believed it, too. He used to dream of new ways to move in a fight. He **claimed** that these moves helped him surprise other fighters. Srinivasa Ramanujan, an important mathematician[3] from India, was a great believer in dreams. He said all his **discoveries** came to him that way. Scientists and writers report getting ideas from dreams, too. The English writer Mary Shelley did. She said that the story of Frankenstein came to her in a dream.

4   Scientists don't agree on what dreams mean or why people dream. Some say that dreams have no meaning and no **purpose**. They say dreams show **activity** in the brain, but it's like the activity of a car going in circles with no driver. It doesn't do anything useful. **On the other hand**, some scientists claim that dreams are **helpful**. They say

continued

[1] a *composer* = a writer of music

[2] a *boxer*

[3] a *mathematician* = someone who does research in math

dreams are good for learning new skills and developing strong memories.

5   Some researchers hope to learn more about people's dreams by studying the dreams of animals. At the Massachusetts Institute of Technology (MIT), scientists have studied the dreams of rats. During the day, the rats were learning to run through a maze.[4] The scientists made pictures of the activity in the rats' brains. Then, during REM sleep, the rats' brains showed exactly the same activity. The rats were going through the maze again in their dreams. Researchers could tell if the dreaming rats were running or standing **still**. In fact, MIT researcher Matthew Wilson reported, "We can pinpoint[5] where they would be in the maze if they were awake."

6   Were the rats practicing for the next day? Does dreaming **somehow** help them learn and remember? Do human brains work this way? Wilson and his team **are searching** for the answers to these questions. Right now, we have no good **explanation** for dreams. There is a lot we don't know about the sleeping brain. Maybe one day we will know all its secrets.

Matthew Wilson's words come from an article by Sarah Smith, "Caught in a Maze," *Psychology Today* 34, no. 3 (May 2001), 20.

[4] a rat in a *maze*

[5] *pinpoint* = show exactly where something is without any mistake

QUICK COMPREHENSION CHECK

Read these sentences. Circle T (true) or F (false).

1. Bruno Beckham says sleep helps him make decisions.   T   F

2. Many people think dreams help us.   T   F

3. According to some famous people, good ideas come in dreams.   T   F

4. Scientists all agree: There are two basic reasons why we dream.   T   F

5. Scientists say dreams are bad for your brain.   T   F

6. Only human beings dream.   T   F

EXPLORING VOCABULARY

Thinking about the Vocabulary

Look at the target words and phrases. Which ones are new to you? Circle
them here and in the reading. Then read "In Your Dreams" again. Look at
the context of each new word and phrase. Can you guess the meaning?

Target Words and Phrases			
right away (1)	useful (2)	purpose (4)	still (5)
whether or not (1)	daily (3)	activity (4)	somehow (6)
whenever (1)	claimed (3)	on the other hand (4)	are searching (6)
cultures (2)	discoveries (3)	helpful (4)	explanation (6)

Using the Vocabulary

 A These sentences are **about the reading**. Complete them with the words
and phrases in the box.

activity	are searching	claimed	cultures	explanation
on the other hand	somehow	still	useful	whenever
whether or not				

1. Bruno doesn't know _____ to accept his new job offer. He can
   choose to accept it or not.

2. Every time that he faces a big decision, Bruno sleeps on it. This means,
   _____ Bruno has a big decision to make, he waits until
   morning.

3. People in different countries have different _____. They
   have their own ways of doing things—their own art, music, religious
   beliefs, etc.

4. Many people believe something _____ happens while we
   sleep, something that helps us.

5. The boxer Floyd Patterson _____ that his dreams helped him
   win fights. Was it true? No one knows for sure. However, this is what
   he said.

6. Dreams show _____ in the brain. Something is happening there.

7. Some scientists say that dreams have no effect on us. _____, there is research showing that dreams help us learn and remember.

8. Sometimes the rats moved through the maze. At other times, they stood _____.

9. Did dreaming help the rats in some way? Did it _____ help them remember where to go in the maze?

10. The researchers at MIT _____ for answers to the question "Why do we dream?" They are trying to find answers.

11. Right now, no one can really explain dreams. We have no good _____ for them.

B These sentences use the target words and phrases **in new contexts.** Complete them with the words and phrases in the box.

activity	claimed	culture	explanation	on the other hand
searched for	somehow	still	useful	whenever
whether or not				

1. The police _____ the missing child.

2. You must sit _____ when I take your picture.

3. She couldn't decide _____ to cut her hair.

4. In general, the stores are busier _____ it rains.

5. I don't know how he did it, but _____, he managed to win.

6. He's so busy that he never seems to sit down! His days are full of _____.

7. I don't understand why she was so upset. Did she give you any _____?

8. You want to store _____ facts in long-term memory so that you'll remember them later.

9. Their _____ teaches them not to show their emotions in public.

10. Bob _____ that his dog could read his mind, but I think he was imagining things.

11. Chris has two job offers. The first one pays better; _____ the second one sounds more secure. A secure job **vs.** a better-paying one—which is more important?

> **Common Abbreviations**
>
> The abbreviation *vs.* is short for the Latin word *versus.* It means "as opposed to or against." This abbreviation is often used for two things being compared, two sports teams going against each other, or the two sides in a court case.

C Read each definition and look at the paragraph number in parentheses ( ). Look back at the reading to **find the target word or phrase** for each definition. Write it in the chart.

Definition	Target Word or Phrase
1. happening very soon, immediately (1)	
2. happening every day (3)	
3. new facts, or answers to questions, that someone learns (3)	
4. a reason for happening or for doing something (4)	
5. useful, good for something (4)	

Building on the Vocabulary

Studying Collocations

The word **right** means "immediately" or "very soon" when it is used with certain other words. Look at these examples of phrases with *right:*

- *I need the money **right away.***
- *I'm coming **right back.** / I'll be **right back.***
- *We're leaving **right now.***

Write three sentences using the three phrases above with *right*.

1. _____

2. _____

3. _____

DEVELOPING YOUR SKILLS

Fact vs. Opinion

 Decide if each statement is a fact or an opinion. Base your answers on information from the reading. Circle *Fact* when it is possible to show that the statement is true. Circle *Opinion* when people may believe it, but they can't show that it is true.

1. There is activity in the brain while we sleep.   Fact /Opinion

2. Our dreams are useful.   Fact/Opinion

3. Some famous people have believed in the power of dreams.   Fact/Opinion

4. Dreams help us learn new skills.   Fact/Opinion

5. MIT scientists have studied the dreams of rats.   Fact/Opinion

6. In the future, scientists will discover why we dream.   Fact/Opinion

B Write two sentences.

1. Write a fact about dreams from "In Your Dreams."

_____

_____

2. Write an opinion of your own about dreams.

_____

_____

Summarizing

Write answers to these questions on a piece of paper. Then use your answers to write a summary of the reading. Write your summary as a paragraph.

1. When do people say, "Sleep on it"?
2. Why do they say it?
3. What do some people say dreams can do?
4. What example can you give of dreams being useful to someone?
5. What do scientists say about the meaning and purpose of dreams?
6. Why do scientists study the dreams of animals?
7. What is one possible reason for dreaming?

Sharing Opinions

Talk about these questions in a small group.

1. Is it important to remember and think about your dreams? Why or why not?

2. Would you like someone to tell you the meaning of your dreams? Why or why not?

3. Do you believe people can learn while they sleep? Why or why not?

Using New Words

Work with a partner. Choose five target words or phrases from the list on page 66. On a piece of paper, use each word or phrase in a sentence.

Writing

Choose a topic. Write a paragraph.

1. Whenever Bruno Beckham faces a big decision, he sleeps on it. What do you do? What, or who, helps you make decisions? How?

2. Think about a time when you had to make a choice. What did you decide? How did you make your decision? Do you think it was the right one? Why or why not?

Wrap-up

REVIEWING VOCABULARY

A Which of the words below can describe a person? There are five correct answers. The first one has been marked for you. Check four more boxes.

A person can be . . .

- ☑ awake.
- ☐ feed.
- ☐ upset.
- ☐ creative.
- ☐ luckily.
- ☐ weak.
- ☐ daily.
- ☐ smart.
- ☐ weight.

B Think about the type of words in each of these groups. Are they nouns, verbs, or adjectives? Cross out the word that does not belong in each group.

1. helpful   ~~somehow~~   deep   active
2. region   period   purpose   alike
3. closet   realize   create   look up
4. emotion   activity   anymore   culture

C Complete the sentences below. There is one extra word or phrase.

according to	concerns	contain	in fact	meant
on the other hand	rate	right away	set	whether or not

1. I don't know _____ I'll go. I have to decide.
2. There is a complete _____ of tools in that box.
3. The doctor listened to the patient's heart _____.
4. Call if you need help, and I'll come _____.
5. Tea doesn't _____ as much caffeine as coffee.
6. I'm a little tired. _____, I think I'll go to bed.
7. _____ the weather report, the rain should end soon.
8. He had a lot of homework. That _____ he couldn't go out.
9. His research _____ the connections between sleep and memory.

EXPANDING VOCABULARY

A A **prefix** is a word part added to the beginning of a word. It changes the word's meaning. Study the chart below.

Prefix	Meaning	Examples
dis-	not or opposite of	*dis*agree, *dis*appear, *dis*connect
ex-	was in the past, but not now	*ex*-boss, *ex*-boyfriend, *ex*-wife
re-	again or back	*re*create, *re*supply, *re*train

Add the correct prefix to the word in parentheses, and use the new word.

1. (agree) Researchers _____*disagree*_____ about the purpose of dreams. They have different ideas about why we dream.

2. (wife) He and his _____ never speak to each other.

3. (supply) The truck carried water to _____ the firefighters.

4. (connect) The phone isn't working. Did someone _____ it?

5. (create) The artist is trying to _____ the work that was destroyed in the fire.

6. (appear) When you visit, my cats _____. They're afraid of you.

B A **suffix** is a word part added to the end of a word to make a new word. The new word is often a different part of speech. For example, the suffix *-tion* (also *-sion* or *-ion*) added to a verb often creates a noun. Sometimes the noun has a change in the spelling of the **stem** or **root** (the main part of the word).

Choose the word that completes the sentence correctly.

1. (connect, connection) Two bridges across the river _____ the towns on either side.

2. (create, creation) Which plan will _____ more jobs?

3. (divide, division) It is easy to _____ an orange into pieces.

4. (explain, explanation) Did he give any _____ for his actions?

5. (invent, invention) The telephone was a great _____.

6. (pronounce, pronunciation) I know the meaning of the word but I'm not sure of its _____.

PLAYING WITH WORDS

There are 12 target words from Unit 2 in this puzzle. The words go across
(→) and down (↓). Find the words and circle them. Then use them to
complete the sentences below.

```
A  X  Z  P  U  R  P  O  S  E
M  I  N  C  L  U  D  E  T  T
O  S  T  I  L  L  A  X  O  Q
U  D  I  S  C  O  V  E  R  Y
N  D  K  W  T  W  E  K  E  S
T  X  V  M  E  K  R  M  Z  E
S  I  N  C  R  E  A  S  E  R
X  Z  H  B  M  Z  G  X  H  I
S  U  P  P  L  Y  E  Z  R  E
W  W  H  E  N  E  V  E  R  S
```

1. They have a big family, so they buy food in large ____amounts____ .

2. Why do we have to do this work? What's the _____ of it?

3. In the summer, I _____ my winter clothes in the back of my closet.

4. Does the price _____ the tax, or do we have to add that?

5. Stand _____ so that I can take your picture.

6. There is an _____ of two children in each family.

7. The scientist explained her _____ to reporters.

8. They worry about the long-_____ effects of this change.

9. After a long _____ of meetings, they came to an agreement.

10. The boss promised us an _____ in pay.

11. Parents try to _____ their children with everything they need.

12. Come _____ you want. We'll be home all day.

BUILDING DICTIONARY SKILLS

Finding Words in the Dictionary, Part 2

Sometimes it is easy to find the word you are looking for in the dictionary. For example, look at *immediately* below. It follows *immediate*. Each word has its own entry in the dictionary. Sometimes a word does not have its own entry. For example, look for *emotionally* below.

---

im·me·di·ate /ɪˈmidiɪt/ *adj* **1** happening or done at once with no delay: *Police deman-ded the immediate release of the hostages.* **2** existing now, and needing to be dealt with quickly: *Our immediate concern was to stop the fire from spreading.* **3** near something or someone in time or place: *We have no plans to expand the business in the immediate future.* **4 immediate family** your parents, children, brothers, and sisters
im·me·di·ate·ly /ɪˈmidiɪtli/ *adv* **1** at once and with no delay: *Mandy answered the phone immediately.* **2** very near to something in time or place: *We left immediately after-wards.* | *They live immediately above us.*

---

e·mo·tion·al /ɪˈmoʊʃənəl/ *adj* **1** making people have strong feelings: *The end of the movie was really emotional.* **2** showing your emotions to other people, especially by crying: *Please don't get all emotional.* **3** relating to your feelings or how they are con-trolled: *the emotional development of children* **4** influenced by what you feel rather than what you know: *an emotional response to the problem* **–emotionally** *adv*
e·mo·tive /ɪˈmoʊtɪv/ *adj* making people have strong feelings: *an emotive speech about the effects of war*

The adverb *emotionally* does not have its own entry. Adverbs ending in *-ly* are often at the end of adjective entries. Other kinds of words also can come at the end of entries.

1. Circle the adverb form of *lucky* below.

2. Circle words related to *useful* at the end of the entry below.

---

luck·y /ˈlʌki/ *adj* **1** having good luck; fortunate: *He's lucky to still be alive.* | *"I just got the last bus." "That was lucky!"* **2 I'll be lucky if** SPOKEN said when you think something is very unlikely: *I'll be lucky if I can pay my bills this month.* **–luckily** *adv*: *Luckily, no one was hurt.*
–opposite UNLUCKY **–see usage note at** LUCK[1]

---

use·ful /ˈyusfəl/ *adj* helping you to do or to get what you want: *use-ful information* | *a useful book for travelers* **–usefully** *adv*
–usefulness *n* [U]

---

3. Fill in the word family chart for *useful*. Then write two sentences with members of this word family.

Noun	Verb	Adjective	Adverb
	use		

a. _____

b. _____

UNIT 3
COMMUNICATION

CHAPTER 9

Who Does It Better?

African elephants—in conversation?

GETTING READY TO READ

Talk with a partner or in a small group.

Do human beings and animals communicate in each of the ways listed below? Circle *Yes* or *No.* For each *yes* answer, give an example.

	Words	Sounds	Movements	Smells
Humans	(Yes) *Hello* No	Yes No	Yes No	Yes No
Animals	Yes No	Yes No	Yes No	Yes No

Share your answers with the rest of the class.

READING

Look at the words and pictures next to the reading. Then read without stopping. Don't worry about new words. Don't stop to use a dictionary. Just keep reading!

Who Does It Better?

1   Who is better at communicating, people or animals? If you think about human inventions such as the telephone, the radio, and the Internet, then the answer to this question seems clear. Human beings are "The Great Communicators." However, think about your own **personal** communication skills. If you compare what you can do with the abilities of certain animals, then the answer is not so simple. Animals can do some things that people cannot.

2   We humans depend on our **voices** for much of our communication. We use words and sounds to pass information to the people around us. But the sound of our voices cannot travel very far. Even the voice of an opera singer[1] with years of training cannot be heard as well as many animal voices. Think of the elephant, for example. Its voice has great **strength** because of the elephant's great size, so it can be heard for miles. Elephants can also make very **low** sounds, sounds that are too deep for any human to hear. These low sounds let elephants communicate over even longer distances. The sounds travel in sound **waves** through the air and through the **ground**. How do elephants receive messages like these? No one knows. Maybe they hear them with their ears, or maybe they **sense** them in some other way. It is possible that these sound waves pass from the ground through the elephants' toenails[2] into their bones and then to their brains!

3   Let's also consider communication **through** movement. For example, some people use dance to share ideas or emotions. When we watch these dancers, we may understand what they are thinking or feeling. But even a great dancer's ability to speak through movement can't match the average honeybee's.[3] Bees do a very special dance to tell other bees where to find food. The dance tells the other bees which way to go so that they can fly in a **straight** line to the food. It also tells them exactly how far to go. It gives clear

[1] an *opera singer*

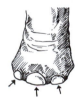

[2] an elephant's *toenails*

[3] a *honeybee*

continued

information about both the **direction** and the distance to a **specific** place.

4   Many animals communicate through smells. A smell can carry a lot of information. For example, a smell can say, "This is my place—get out!" or a smell can give an **invitation**. Often a **female** animal who wants a **male** to come to her will produce a smell to **attract** him. It says to the male, "Here I am—come and find me." Many animals receive messages through their noses just as humans do. For example, your nose might tell you, "There's fresh coffee in the kitchen. It's time to get out of bed." But people don't usually use smells to communicate, and our noses don't receive messages very well. We certainly can't **compete** with the Great White Shark.[4] A large part of its brain—14% of it—is just for "reading" smells in the ocean.

5   Our noses are not the best, our voices are not the strongest, and our dancing may not say anything at all. But people are the only ones with words and written languages. So, maybe we can still say we are "The Great Communicators."

[4] a *Great White Shark*

Quick Comprehension Check

Read these sentences. Circle T (true) or F (false).

1.	Humans communicate better than animals in every way.	T	F
2.	Elephants can make sounds that travel far.	T	F
3.	Bees can communicate with other bees through movement.	T	F
4.	A honeybee dances to tell other bees about danger.	T	F
5.	Both animals and people use their noses to get information.	T	F
6.	The Great White Shark is good at "reading" smells in the ocean.	T	F

EXPLORING VOCABULARY

Thinking about the Vocabulary

Which target words are new to you? Circle them here and in the reading. Then read "Who Does It Better?" again. Look at the context of each new word. Can you guess the meaning?

Target Words

personal (1)	**waves** (2)	**straight** (3)	**female** (4)
voices (2)	**ground** (2)	**direction** (3)	**male** (4)
strength (2)	**sense** (2)	**specific** (3)	**attract** (4)
low (2)	**through** (3)	**invitation** (4)	**compete** (4)

Using the Vocabulary

A Complete the sentences. Write *female, ground, straight,* and *waves.*

1. She's sitting on the
   _____.

2. _____ birds
   lay eggs.

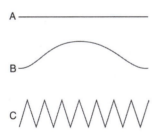

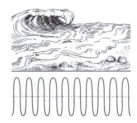

3. Only line A is _____.

4. Here are ocean _____
   and sound waves.

B These sentences are **about the reading**. Complete them with the words in the box.

attract	compete	direction	invitation	low	male
personal	sense	specific	strength	through	voice

1. Each person has his or her own _____ communication skills. These are the skills that belong to that one person.

2. When you speak or sing, you use your _____. Other people hear it.

3. An elephant has great _____. This means an elephant is very strong.

4. Elephants sometimes make sounds that are not high enough for the human ear to hear. These are very _____ sounds. (Other animals, such as dogs, can hear sounds that are too high for human ears.)

5. Elephants hear with their ears. Maybe they also _____ sounds through their toenails. It is not clear how they receive some very low sounds.

6. Some animals, like bees, communicate _____ movement. They use movement.

7. The bee's dance tells other bees the _____ to fly in (which way to go) and also how far to go to find food.

8. A bee can tell other bees how to get to a _____ place—that is, one certain place.

9. A smell can mean "Go away!" or it can give an _____, a friendly offer like, "Come and be with me!"

10. A female animal may produce a smell to get the attention of a _____ animal. She wants him to know she is there.

11. When a female wants a male to come to her, she tries to _____ him, or make him interested in her.

12. Humans should not try to _____ with the Great White Shark as far as the ability to smell is concerned. The shark would always win.

These sentences use the target words in new contexts. Complete them with the words in the box.

attracted	compete	direction	invitation	low	male
personal	sensed	specific	strength	through	voices

1. I was upset about not getting an _____ to the party.

2. "Put it in *a* closet" means in any closet, but "Put it in *the* closet" means in one _____ closet.

3. The scientist made his discoveries _____ years of hard work.

4. At night, the light _____ insects, so we turned it off.

5. She turned the car around and drove off in the opposite _____.

6. She didn't say anything, but I _____ that something was wrong.

7. Men usually have lower _____ than women do.

8. He has learned about the business world both in school and through his own _____ experience.

9. Athletes from many countries _____ at the Olympic games. Each person tries to win.

10. He was so sick he didn't have the _____ to get out of bed.

11. _____ animals are often larger than female animals of the same kind.

12. A piano makes _____ sounds when you play the keys on the left end.

←low notes   high notes→

Building on the Vocabulary

Studying Word Grammar

The word *low* is usually an adjective. It can describe:

- a quiet or deep sound: *a low whisper, a low voice*
- something that isn't high or tall: *a low wall, a low building*
- a small amount or number: *low-fat food, low grades*
- the bad nature of something: *a low opinion, a low trick*

Low can also be:

- an adverb (*The plane was flying low.*)
- a noun (*Prices fell to a new low.*)

A **Is *low* a noun, an adjective, or an adverb in each sentence? Circle your answers.**

1. The TV sits on a low table.   *n. / adj. / adv.*
2. Everybody's life has its highs and lows.   *n. / adj. / adv.*
3. Shoppers like low prices.   *n. / adj. / adv.*
4. He threw the ball low.   *n. / adj. / adv.*
5. I got a low score on the test.   *n. / adj. / adv.*

B **Write four sentences using *low* in four different ways.**

1. _____

   _____

2. _____

   _____

3. _____

   _____

4. _____

   _____

DEVELOPING YOUR SKILLS

Reading for Details

Read these sentences. Then reread "Who Does It Better?" for the answers. If the reading doesn't give the information, check (✓) *It doesn't say.*

	True	False	It doesn't say.
1. We depend on our voices for much of our communication with other people.			
2. Elephants have the best hearing of any animals.			
3. Sound waves can travel only through the air.			
4. The dance of the honeybee tells other bees which way to go to find food.			
5. The dance of the honeybee tells other bees what kind of food they will find.			
6. All living things use smells to communicate.			
7. Most of a Great White Shark's brain is used for reading smells in the ocean.			
8. Words give human beings a very special way to communicate.			

Understanding Main Ideas and Supporting Details

A Match the main ideas and the details that support them. Write the letters.

Main Ideas	Supporting Details
_c_ 1. Certain inventions help people communicate.	a. Bees do a dance to tell other bees where food is.
_____ 2. The human voice can't travel as far as some animal voices.	b. A female animal may produce a smell to attract a male.
_____ 3. Some animals communicate through movement.	c. Think of the telephone, the radio, and the Internet.
_____ 4. Animals sometimes use smells to communicate with other animals.	d. The Great White Shark has a much better sense of smell than we do.
_____ 5. People can't compete with animals in some ways.	e. An elephant's voice can be heard for miles.

Think of another example to support each general statement in Part A. Write complete sentences.

1. <u>Inventions like pens and paper let people write to each other.</u>

2. _____

3. _____

4. _____

5. _____

Discussion

Talk about these questions in a small group.

1. According to the reading, people don't usually communicate through smell. But what are people saying when they put on something that smells good, such as perfume, cologne, or aftershave?

2. In what ways do people and animals communicate with each other? Think of at least three examples.

Using New Words

Work with a partner. Take turns asking and answering these questions. Then tell the class something your partner said.

1. Who has **straight** hair?
2. What singer's **voice** do you like?
3. What are three ways to build up your **strength**?
4. When or where do you sit on the **ground**?
5. How would you complete this sentence? *I would like an **invitation** to . . .*

Writing

Choose a topic. Write a paragraph.

1. Pets sometimes play an important part in people's lives. People communicate with their pets in several ways. Have you ever had a pet? How do or did you communicate?

2. What kind of animal would you like to be? Why? Tell both the good and the bad things about being this kind of animal.

3. Imagine that you are an animal. Describe a day in your life.

CHAPTER 10

When and Why We Laugh

A room full of laughter

GETTING READY TO READ

Talk in a small group or with the whole class.

1. Look at the picture. Which person is laughing "in English"? What about the others? Do you see a word that is used in your first language to show laughter?

2. Ask one person in your group to make himself or herself laugh. Then talk about what happened in your group when this person laughed, or tried to.

3. How many people in your group are ticklish?[1]

[1] *ticklish* = easily made to laugh when someone touches certain parts of your body

READING

Look at the words and picture next to the reading. Then read without stopping.

When and Why We Laugh

1   People have many ways to **express** themselves—to show how they feel or what they think. One way that feels especially good is **laughter**. We laugh when we see or hear something funny, and we laugh sometimes just because other people are laughing. Some people laugh when someone tickles[1] them. Laughter has an important place in human communication. The question is, what are we saying when we laugh?

2   A team of psychologists[2] studied the laughter of 120 students at an American university. They had the students watch funny movies. Sometimes the students were alone, and sometimes they were in pairs. The psychologists **recorded** the students' laughter, and they **noticed** that the students made a wide **variety** of laughing sounds. They found that there were differences both in how a student laughed and in how many times the student laughed. Both these things depended on his or her partner. Was the other person the same sex or the opposite sex? And what was the **relationship** between the two? Was the person a friend or a **stranger**? Here are some of the researchers' findings:[3]

- Men laughed much more during the movies when they were with a friend. The friend could be male or female. They laughed much less when their partner was a stranger or when they were alone.

- Women laughed most with men friends.

- Women laughed in a higher voice with male strangers.

- There were three basic types of laughs: high song-like laughs, laughs with the sounds coming mostly through the nose, and low grunting[4] laughs like the sounds a pig makes.

3   In another **study**, the researchers asked people to listen to these three types of laughter. They wanted to know which kind people liked best. They asked questions like: Does the person laughing sound friendly? Do you think he or she

continued

[1] *tickle* = touch certain parts of someone's body to make him or her laugh

[2] a *psychologist* = someone trained in the study of the mind and how it works

[3] *findings* = the information that someone learns as a result of research

[4] A pig makes low *grunting* sounds.

sounds **attractive**? Would you like to meet this person? Most people **preferred** the high song-like sounds. They were attracted to people who laughed this way.

4   The researchers believe that laughter is a tool we use, usually without thinking about it. They say we use it to influence the emotions and **behavior** of other people. We often use it to show that we want to be friends. In fact, most laughter during conversation is *not* because we are listening to something funny. Researcher Robert Provine says that in conversation, listeners **actually** laugh less than speakers do. The speakers' laughter has a social[5] purpose. Provine calls laughter "the **oil** in the social machine." **In other words**, it helps relationships between people work **smoothly**.

[5] *social* = relating to living together in groups

5   Did you know that humans are not the only ones who laugh? Dogs do, too. Dog laughter sounds something like "Huh, huh, huh." It seems to express the idea "Let's play!" Another university researcher, Jaak Panksepp, reports that rats laugh, too. They laugh when he tickles them. But please don't go out and try this. Panksepp **warns**, "You have to know the rat."

Robert Provine's words come from "He Who Laughs Less?" *PBS—Scientific American Frontiers: Life's Little Questions II,* <www.pbs.org/saf>. Jaak Panksepp was quoted in "Don't Look Now, But Is That Dog Laughing?" *Science News* 160, no. 4 (July 28, 2001), 55.

Quick Comprehension Check

Read these sentences. Circle T (true) or F (false).

1. Laughter is part of human communication.   T   F

2. Researchers study why and how people laugh.   T   F

3. The people who are with us affect how we laugh.   T   F

4. The college students in the study laughed only with their   T   F
   friends.

5. Researchers say that we laugh to influence other people.   T   F

6. Only human beings laugh.   T   F

EXPLORING VOCABULARY

Thinking about the Vocabulary

Which target words and phrases are new to you? Circle them here and in the reading. Then read "When and Why We Laugh" again. Look at the context of each new word and phrase. Can you guess the meaning?

Target Words and Phrases			
express (1)	variety (2)	attractive (3)	oil (4)
laughter (1)	relationship (2)	preferred (3)	in other words (4)
recorded (2)	stranger (2)	behavior (4)	smoothly (4)
noticed (2)	study (3)	actually (4)	warns (5)

Using the Vocabulary

 These sentences are **about the reading.** Complete them with the words and phrases in the box.

actually	behavior	express	in other words	laughter	noticed
preferred	relationship	studies	variety	warned	

1. People communicate ideas and emotions with words. We can also
    _____ ourselves with sounds.

2. The sound of _____ sometimes makes other people laugh,
    too.

3. The researchers _____, or realized, that the students laughed
    differently.

4. Not everyone laughs the same way. People make a _____ of
    sounds.

5. Researchers studied the laughter of pairs of students. It was important to
    consider the _____, or connection, between the two
    students—that is, how well they knew each other.

6. Scientists do _____ to find the answers to research questions.
    Then they write reports on their results.

7. In one study, people listened to three types of laughter and chose the one they liked best. Most people _____ the same type.

8. Researchers say we use laughter to influence the _____ of other people—that is, to influence what they do and say.

9. Who laughs more in conversation, the speaker or the listener? Most people would guess "the listener," but _____, it is the speaker.

10. You can use the phrase "_____" to mean "Here is another way to say the same thing." Often the second way is easier to understand.

11. One researcher said to be careful about tickling rats. He _____ people to be careful.

B These sentences use the target words and phrases **in new contexts.** Complete them with the words and phrases in the box.

actually	behavior	expresses	in other words	laughter	notice
prefer	relationship	study	variety	warns	

1. The room was full of the sounds of music, conversation, and _____.

2. The teacher called the boy's parents to talk about his bad _____.

3. The sign _____ drivers that the road is bad, so they should be careful.

4. He likes his boss. They have a friendly _____.

5. What would you _____ to do, go to a movie or go out to eat?

6. She claimed to be 21, but she was _____ 19.

7. He almost never _____ his feelings or talks about anything personal.

8. I walked past the car, but I didn't _____ if anyone was in it.

9. The college offers a wide _____ of courses. There are a lot of choices for students.

10. The scientists were interested in the effects of sleep on memory, so they did a _____.

11. This street is a dead end. _____, it doesn't connect with another street, so you can't drive through.

C Read each definition and look at the paragraph number in parentheses ( ).
Look back at the reading to **find the target word** for each definition. Write
it in the chart.

Definition	Target Word
1. a person you do not know (2)	
2. stored music or other sound so as to be able to hear it again (2)	
3. nice or pleasing to look at, interesting (3)	
4. a liquid used to help machine parts move easily (4)	
5. happening without problems or difficulties (4)	

Building on the Vocabulary

Studying Collocations

Prepositions, such as *at, in,* and *to,* help show relationships between people,
places, and things. Certain prepositions follow certain adjectives. Use:

> *attractive + to*   *upset + about*
> *excited + about*   *useful + for/to*
> *interested + in*

Example: *I am excited about our trip.*

A Complete each sentence with the correct preposition.

1. He wrote a book that's useful _____ travelers visiting Japan.

2. The children were excited _____ getting your invitation.

3. Chris is very attractive _____ the opposite sex.

4. Everyone was upset _____ the accident.

5. I'm interested _____ learning about other cultures.

B Write five sentences. Use each adjective + preposition in Part A.

1. _____

2. _____

3. _____

4. _____

5. _____

DEVELOPING YOUR SKILLS

Finding Clues to Meaning

Writers use a variety of ways to supply the meaning of a word or phrase in a reading.

- Sometimes a writer follows the word or phrase with a comma (,) or a dash (—) and then a definition or explanation. For example, "Mahmoud was born near Tehran, the largest city in Iran." or "This body part is small—only 2–3% of your total body weight—but it uses . . ."

- Sometimes a phrase like *that is* or *in other words* introduces a definition or explanation. For example, "Does the information affect our emotions? That is, does it make us happy, sad, excited, or upset?"

Look at "When and Why We Laugh." Find the definitions or explanations given for the boldfaced phrases below and copy them here.

1. "People have many ways to **express themselves** _____

   _____"

2. "Provine calls laughter '**the oil in the social machine**.' _____

   _____"

Reading for Details

Read these questions about "When and Why We Laugh." Refer back to the reading and write short answers or complete sentences.

1. What are three reasons for laughter?

   a. _____

   b. _____

   c. _____

2. Who did a study on laughter? _____

3. Who was in the study? _____

4. What did the students have to do? _____

   _____

5. What did changes in the students' laughter depend on? _____

   _____

6. When did the female students in the study laugh most? _____

7. When did the male students laugh most? _____

8. According to researcher Robert Provine, who laughs more during a conversation, the person speaking or the one listening? _____

9. **a.** What does Provine call laughter? (Use Provine's exact words to answer this question.) _____

   b. What does this mean? _____

Discussion

Work with a partner. Talk about your answers to these questions.

1. Research on laughter shows that the average adult laughs about 17 times a day. How many times do you think you laugh during the day? What kinds of things make you laugh?

2. What do you think is the difference between "laughing at someone" and "laughing with someone"?

3. According to the reading, the female college students in the study
   a. laughed most with male friends and
   b. laughed in a higher voice with male strangers.

   Why do you think they laughed like this?

Using New Words

Work with a partner. Choose five target words or phrases from the list on page 89. On a piece of paper, use each word or phrase in a sentence.

Writing

Choose a topic. Write a paragraph.

1. Some people say, "Laughter is the best medicine." Do you agree? Why or why not?

2. "Laughter is the best medicine" is a common saying in English. Think of a common saying about laughter in your first language. Tell what it is, what it means, and why you do or don't agree with it.

CHAPTER 11

The Inventor of the Telephone

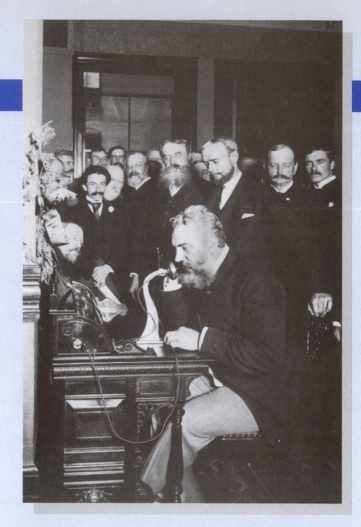

The inventor of the telephone

GETTING READY TO READ

Mark your answers to the following questions. Then discuss your answers in a small group or with the whole class.

1. Who invented the telephone?

   ❏ Thomas Edison   ❏ Guglielmo Marconi   ❏ Alexander Graham Bell

2. How many times a day do you usually use a telephone?

   ❏ 0–2 times   ❏ 3–10 times   ❏ more than 10 times

3. Which of the following communication tools do you use regularly?

   At home: Away from home:

   ❏ a telephone   ❏ a cell phone

   ❏ an answering machine   ❏ pay phones

   ❏ other: _____   ❏ other: _____

READING

Look at the words and pictures next to the reading. Then read without stopping.

The Inventor of the Telephone

1   We can thank Alexander Graham Bell for the telephone. This great inventor was born in 1847 in Scotland. All through his life, Bell had an interest in communication. This interest came **partly** from the influence of his family. His grandfather was an actor and became famous as a **speech** teacher. His father developed the first international phonetic alphabet.[1] For his mother, communication was never easy. It took a great **effort** because she was almost completely **deaf**. She usually held a tube[2] to her ear **in order to** hear people. Her son Alexander discovered another way to communicate with her when he was a little boy. He used to **press** his mouth against her forehead[3] and speak in a low voice. The sound waves traveled to her ears through the bones of her head. This was among the first of his many discoveries about sound.

2   As a teenager, Bell taught music and public speaking at a boys' school. In his free time, he had fun working on **various** inventions with an older brother. These included a useful machine for farmwork. Then both of Bell's brothers got sick and died. He got the same terrible **sickness**— tuberculosis[4]—so the family moved to Canada. There his health returned.

3   Bell moved to the United States when he was 24. He went to Boston to teach at a school for deaf children. In Boston, he fell in love with Mabel Hubbard, a student of his who later became his wife. During this period of his life, Bell was a very busy man. **In addition to** teaching, he was working on several inventions.

4   Bell's main goal was to make machines to help deaf people hear. He was also trying to build a better telegraph.[5] In those days, the telegraph was the only way to send information quickly over a long distance. Telegraph messages traveled over **wires**. They were sent in Morse code,[6] which used specific long and short sounds for the letters of the

continued

[1] a *phonetic alphabet* = a way to show the sounds of words, for example *laugh* = /læf/ or (läf)

[2] a hearing *tube*

[3] *forehead*

[4] *tuberculosis* = a serious sickness that affects a person's ability to breathe

[5] a *telegraph* operator sending a message

[6] *Morse code* for SOS, a call for help

· · · — — — · · ·

alphabet. Bell was trying to find a way to send the human voice along a wire. However, almost no one believed in this idea, and people told him, "You're **wasting** your time. You should try to invent a better telegraph—that's where the money is."

5   Bell understood a lot about sound and **electricity**, but he wasn't really very **good at** building things. Luckily, he met someone who was. The man's name was Thomas Watson, and he was a great help to Bell. One day—it was March 10, 1876—the two men were working in **separate** rooms. They were getting ready to test a new invention, which had a wire going from one room to the other. Something **went wrong** and Bell **shouted**, "Mr. Watson, come here. I want you!" His voice traveled along the wire, and Watson heard it coming from the new machine. It was the world's first telephone call. Bell was on his way to becoming a very rich man.

6   Soon afterward, Bell wrote to his father:

> The day is coming when telegraph wires will [go] to houses just like water or gas—and friends will converse with each other without leaving home.

Maybe his father laughed to hear this idea. At the time, most people expected the phone to be just a tool for business, not something that anyone would have at home. Bell could see a greater future for it. However, even he could probably never imagine what telephones are like today.

The quotation from Alexander Graham Bell's letter to his father comes from "Alexander Graham Bell—The Inventor," <http://www.fitzgeraldstudio.com/html/bell/inventor.html>.

Quick Comprehension Check

Read these sentences. Circle T (true) or F (false).

1. Alexander Graham Bell's family influenced his career.   T   F

2. Bell started inventing things while he was growing up.   T   F

3. He was born and grew up in the United States.   T   F

4. He never married.   T   F

5. He invented the telephone working all alone.   T   F

6. He believed that in the future, people would have phones   T   F
   at home.

EXPLORING VOCABULARY

Thinking about the Vocabulary

Which target words and phrases are new to you? Circle them here and in the reading. Then read "The Inventor of the Telephone" again. Look at the context of each new word and phrase. Can you guess the meaning?

Target Words and Phrases			
partly (1)	in order to (1)	in addition to (3)	good at (5)
speech (1)	press (1)	wires (4)	separate (5)
effort (1)	various (2)	wasting (4)	went wrong (5)
deaf (1)	sickness (2)	electricity (5)	shouted (5)

Using the Vocabulary

 Complete these sentences. Write *a great effort, pressing, shouting,* and *wires.*

1. He's _____.

2. It's taking _____.

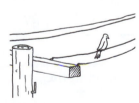

3. These are telephone _____.

4. He's _____ a button.

B These sentences are **about the reading**. Complete them with the words and phrases in the box.

deaf	electricity	good at	in addition to	in order to	partly
separate	sickness	speech	various	waste	went wrong

1. Some, but not all, of Bell's interest in communication was because of his family. It came _____ from their influence on him.

2. Bell's grandfather taught people to speak clearly. He was a _____ teacher.

3. Bell's mother could hear only a little. She was almost completely _____.

4. She used a tube _____ hear people. She used it for this purpose.

5. As a teenager, Bell worked with his brother on _____ inventions. They built a variety of things together.

6. Bell's two brothers got sick and died. Then he got the same _____.

7. Bell had a teaching job in Boston. He also had more to do: _____ his job, he worked on several inventions.

8. People told Bell to use his time carefully. They told him not to _____ his time.

9. Bell understood a lot about _____. For example, he knew how it could supply power to lights.

10. Bell was a great thinker, but he wasn't so _____ building things.

11. On March 10, 1876, Bell and his partner were not working in the same room. They were in _____ rooms.

12. While he was working, Bell had an accident of some kind. Something _____.

These sentences use the target words and phrases **in new contexts**. Complete them with the words and phrases in the box.

deaf	electricity	good at	go wrong	in addition to	in order to
partly	separate	sickness	speech	various	waste

1. The sky was only _____ cloudy in the morning but completely cloudy later on.

2. He's going _____. I have to shout so that he can hear me.

3. This type of car is available in _____ colors.

4. Michael plays basketball and golf very well. He is _____ both sports.

5. We depend on _____ for lights, radios, TVs, refrigerators, etc.

6. The company wants a study on how many work days are lost because of _____.

7. Relax! I'm sure everything will go smoothly. Nothing will _____.

8. Don't _____ your money on that movie. We saw it, and it was very disappointing.

9. He took science courses _____ prepare for a career in medicine.

10. I keep my notes for each of my courses in _____ parts of my notebook.

11. Only humans can express themselves through _____.

12. We use laughter to communicate, _____ words, sounds, and body language.

Building on the Vocabulary

Studying Collocations

Remember: Certain verbs go with certain nouns. Use the verbs *make, take,* and *put* with the noun *effort.* Also note that *effort* is sometimes a count noun and sometimes a noncount noun. Study these examples:

- make an effort to do something

- it takes (an/some) effort to do something

- put (some/a lot of) effort into something

A Complete the sentences. Use *make, put,* or *take.*

1. Does it _____ a lot of effort to learn a language?
2. Please _____ an effort to be on time.
3. He won't _____ any effort into his homework.

B Write three sentences with *make, put,* and *take + effort.*

1. _____
2. _____
3. _____

DEVELOPING YOUR SKILLS

Reading Between the Lines

Are the following statements true or false? You cannot skim the reading for the answers. You must think about what the reading says and decide. Circle T or F, and give one or more reasons for your answer. Write complete sentences.

1. Alexander Graham Bell was probably close to his family.　　Ⓣ　　F

   His family influenced his career, and he and his brother invented things
   together.

2. Bell had a fear of speaking in front of groups of people.　　T　　F

   _____

   _____

3. Tuberculosis was a serious sickness in the 1800s.　　T　　F

   _____

   _____

4. Bell's wife was deaf.　　T　　F

   _____

   _____

5. What Bell wanted most in life was to become rich and famous.　　T　　F

   _____

   _____

6. Thomas Watson believed in Bell's ideas when others did not.　　T　　F

   _____

   _____

Summarizing

On a piece of paper, write a summary of "The Inventor of the Telephone."
Use no more than ten sentences. Use your own words. That is, do not
copy sentences from the reading. Include:

- the inventor's name
- why he is famous
- when and where he was born
- where he spent his life
- his main goal as an inventor
- the date of the first phone call

Discussion

Talk about these questions in a small group.

1. How did Alexander Graham Bell's family influence his career?

2. Have you ever spent one or more days in a place where you had no phone
   nearby? If so, where were you? Describe your feelings about being far from
   a phone.

3. Imagine the perfect telephone of the future. What will it be like? What will
   it be able to do?

Using New Words

**Work with a partner. Take turns asking for and giving information. Use
one of the words in parentheses. Then tell the class something your
partner said.**

1. Name a machine (with/without) buttons you **press** to make it work.

2. Name a machine that (uses/doesn't use) **electricity**.

3. Name a machine (with/without) **wires**.

4. Name a place where you can see **various** kinds of (fish/birds).

5. Name a time and place where it is (OK/not OK) to **shout**.

Writing

Choose a topic. Write a paragraph.

1. How important are telephones in your life? Why and how often do you
   make or get phone calls? Write about your relationship with the telephone.

2. Complete this sentence: *I wish somebody would invent. . .* Explain why this
   invention would be a good thing.

CHAPTER 12

Going Online

Online at home

GETTING READY TO READ

Answer the questions. Then talk about your answers with the class.

1. Do you use the Internet?

   ❑ No, I don't.   ❑ Yes, I use it for:

   _____ e-mail   _____ meeting people

   _____ shopping   _____ music

   _____ getting information   _____ other: _____

2. Circle one: (Many/Some/Only a few) people in my country use the Internet.

3. Do you believe the following statement is true or false?
   People who use the Internet a lot don't like to spend time with other people.

102

READING

Look at the words next to the reading. Then read without stopping.

Going Online

1   All over the world, people are **gaining** access[1] to the Internet. More and more people are using computers to go **online**. This change has happened quickly. For example, in 1997, there were fewer than eight million Internet users in Japan. Just five years later, there were almost 65 million. During that same period, Internet use around the world grew by 600%. Clearly, the Internet is affecting many, many lives, and it is changing how we communicate. But are these changes good or bad?

2   The Internet can be a great tool for communication. Everyone agrees on that. People can use e-mail to keep **in touch** with family and friends whether they are far away or just across town. Sending an e-mail message is quick, easy, and **cheap**. People can also use the Internet to find new friends. Do you want to talk about politics[2] or sports or how to find true love? Go online! You will find people who share your interests. Maybe you will make friends in **distant** places and learn about other cultures. In many ways, the Internet can bring people together.

3   However, some people say that the Internet has the opposite effect. They claim that it is leading to *less* communication, not more. These people believe that time online means time alone. "The Internet is taking people away from their families and friends," they say. "It **draws** people away from their **communities**, and that is not good."

4   So, what is actually happening? Researchers are trying to find out. They are studying the effects of the Internet on our lives. They are looking at the behavior of people who use it and people who do not. At this **point**, there are two basic ideas about what is happening:

- Some researchers who have done studies in the United States have bad news for people who often go online. They report that people who use the Internet **on a regular basis** are more often lonely and unhappy. They say that these people are spending time at their

continued

[1] *access* = the ability, chance, or right to use something

[2] *politics* = activities and ideas concerned with getting and using power in a country, city, etc.

computers instead of with other people, so they have less active **social** lives.

- Other researchers disagree. They describe other studies from the United States and some from England. These show that people who often go online make *more* connections with other people because they use the Internet to communicate. And here is a surprise: According to these studies, **frequent** Internet users get in touch more not just online but by phone and in person,[3] too. They have busier social lives, and they are usually happier. They also watch less TV.

[3] *in person* = by going and meeting someone, not by phone, letter, or computer

5   Does going online affect everyone in the same way? Perhaps not. Perhaps the effects of Internet use depend on a person's **character**. Psychologist[4] Robert Kraut thinks this is so. According to Kraut, the Internet **allows** social people to become even more social. It lets them get in touch with friends more easily, and they go out more often. And people who are not social? They may use the Internet to **avoid** others. They may like going online so that they don't have to talk to anyone. However, this does not mean that the Internet is unhealthy for shy people. In fact, the Internet can help **shy** people make friends. Researchers find that shy people frequently communicate more easily online than face-to-face.

[4] a *psychologist* = someone trained in the study of the mind and how it works

6   The Internet is changing how we communicate. Maybe you can see its effects on your own life. It is less easy to see larger changes in our communities or around the **entire** world, but changes are happening. It is something to think about.

Quick Comprehension Check

Read these sentences. Circle T (true) or F (false).

1. Use of the Internet is growing around the world.   T   F

2. Everyone agrees that the Internet is great for families.   T   F

3. There is no research yet on Internet use in people's homes.   T   F

4. Researchers are studying the behavior of people who often go online.   T   F

5. The Internet is changing how people communicate.   T   F

6. The effects of these changes are clear.   T   F

EXPLORING VOCABULARY

Thinking about the Vocabulary

Which target words and phrases are new to you? Circle them here and in the reading. Then read "Going Online" again. Look at the context of each new word and phrase. Can you guess the meaning?

Target Words and Phrases			
gaining (1)	distant (2)	on a regular basis (4)	allows (5)
online (1)	draws (3)	social (4)	avoid (5)
in touch (2)	communities (3)	frequent (4)	shy (5)
cheap (2)	point (4)	character (5)	entire (6)

Using the Vocabulary

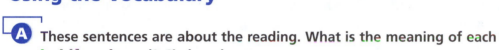 These sentences are about the reading. What is the meaning of each **boldfaced** word? Circle a, b, or c.

1. More and more people are **gaining** experience with the Internet. *Gain* means:

    a. decrease   **b.** imagine   **c.** get

2. Not every computer has a connection to the Internet, but many computers do. People can use those computers to spend time **online**. *Online* means:

    a. in communication with other computers   **b.** using computer hardware   **c.** developing computer games

3. Both e-mail and the telephone let people get **in touch** with friends. *In touch* means:

    a. putting hands on   **b.** in communication   **c.** competing

4. Phone calls can be expensive, but e-mail is **cheap**. *Cheap* means:

    a. a waste of time   **b.** low in cost   **c.** not useful

5. You can send e-mail to people in the same building or in **distant** places. *Distant* means:

    a. far away   **b.** attractive   **c.** specific

6. Some people think time online **draws** people away from others. *Draws* means:

    a. pulls   **b.** rushes   **c.** supplies

7. At this **point**, the effects of the Internet are not yet clear. Here, *point* means:

   a. an idea or belief   **b.** a specific moment   **c.** a reason or
                                       or time   purpose

8. Some people never go online; others use the Internet **on a regular basis**.
   On a regular basis means:

   a. being awake   **b.** moving smoothly   **c.** happening
                                                             often

9. Some Internet users prefer to be alone. Others have busy **social** lives.
   Social means:

   a. relating to other   **b.** relating to research   **c.** relating to
       people   power

10. Some people use the Internet to **avoid** other people because they prefer to
    be alone. *Avoid* means:

    a. make friends with   **b.** keep away from   **c.** spend time
                                                                   with

B These sentences use the target words and phrases **in new contexts.**
Complete them with the words and phrases in the box.

avoid	cheap		distant	draw	gain
in touch	on a regular basis		online	point	social

1. They don't have much money, so they want a _____ used car.

2. He's so thin! He needs to _____ some weight.

3. That child spends too much time alone. He's not developing
   _____ skills.

4. He disappeared at some _____ during the party, but no one
   noticed when.

5. The doctor warned me to _____ high-fat foods.

6. I go _____ for a variety of reasons. For example, I get news
   and weather reports off the Internet.

7. He practices every day. He says, "You need to practice _____
   in order to get better at anything."

8. She dreams of having the money to travel to _____ places.

9. I'd like to _____ your attention to a report in today's
   newspaper.

10. Both *keep* and *stay* _____ *with someone* mean to continue
    communication with the person, usually by phone or by writing.

C Read these sentences. Write the **boldfaced** target words next to their definitions.

a. They lead active social lives. They seem to know everyone in the **community**.

b. He may seem unfriendly at first, but he's actually just **shy**.

c. She used to get headaches every day, but they are becoming less **frequent**.

d. We spent the **entire** day getting ready for the party.

e. The city doesn't **allow** people to smoke in restaurants.

f. He's a stranger to me, so I can't tell you anything about his **character**.

Target Words	Definitions
1. _____	= what a person is like
2. _____	= nervous or uncomfortable about meeting and talking to people
3. _____	= all the people living in a place, or a group that shares an interest
4. _____	= whole, complete
5. _____	= happening very often
6. _____	= let (someone do something)

Building on the Vocabulary

Studying Collocations

Certain verbs are used with certain nouns. For example, the verb *gain* is often used with the nouns *experience, strength,* and *weight*. *Gain* usually means to get more and more of something over a period of time. Similar verbs are *earn* (*money, points*) and *win* (*a game, a prize*).

Complete these sentences with *gain, earn,* or *win*. Use the verb that goes with the noun.

1. The job doesn't pay much, but he'll _____ useful experience.

2. I have to watch what I eat. I _____ weight easily.

3. I hope they'll _____ their next game.

4. You can't _____ much money at most part-time jobs.

5. He's doing exercises to _____ strength in his arms.

DEVELOPING YOUR SKILLS

Pronoun Reference

Pronouns are words like *he, she, it,* or *them. This, that, these,* and *those* can also be pronouns. We often use pronouns to avoid repeating words. A pronoun takes the place of a noun or a noun phrase (a noun phrase = a group of words for a person, place, or thing: *Internet users, the opposite effect*). A pronoun can also refer back to a whole sentence or an idea.

What do the boldfaced pronouns refer to in these sentences? Look back at the reading.

1. Paragraph 2: Everyone agrees on **that**. <u>the idea that the Internet is a</u>
   <u>great tool for communication</u>

2. Paragraph 3: **It** draws people away from their communities . . . _____
   _____

3. Paragraph 4: **They** are studying the effects of the Internet on . . . _____
   _____

4. Paragraph 4: **These** show that people who often go online make *more*
   connections . . . _____

5. Paragraph 4: **They** have busier social lives, and . . . _____

6. Paragraph 5: Psychologist Robert Kraut thinks **this** is so. _____
   _____

Fact vs. Opinion

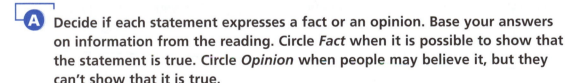

A **Decide if each statement expresses a fact or an opinion. Base your answers on information from the reading. Circle *Fact* when it is possible to show that the statement is true. Circle *Opinion* when people may believe it, but they can't show that it is true.**

1. The Internet has changed how people communicate.   **Fact/Opinion**

2. Use of the Internet has increased in many countries.   **Fact/Opinion**

3. Time spent online makes people less connected to   **Fact/Opinion**
   their communities.

4. Researchers are studying the behavior of Internet users.   **Fact/Opinion**

5. Going online is good for social people.   **Fact/Opinion**

6. Going online is good for shy people.   **Fact/Opinion**

B **Write two sentences.**

1. Write a fact about the Internet from "Going Online."

_____

2. Write an opinion of your own about Internet use.

_____

Discussion

Talk about these questions in a small group.

1. When did you, or will you, learn to use the Internet? How did you, or will you, learn about it?
2. Celine Adams is a grandmother in Canada. Her children just got her a computer. They live far away, and she is excited about getting e-mail from them. But she worries, "Will they stop calling me? I still want to hear their voices." After reading "Going Online," what would you tell Celine? Why?

Using New Words

Work with a partner. Choose five target words or phrases from the list on page 105. On a piece of paper, use each word or phrase in a sentence.

Writing

Choose a topic. Write a paragraph.

1. Do you feel that you are part of a community at school, at work, or where you live? If so, how would you describe this community? How does it feel to be a part of it?
2. Do you keep in touch with friends or family in distant places? Tell why or why not. Explain how you stay in touch or what keeps you from staying in touch.

Wrap-up

REVIEWING VOCABULARY

 A Match the words in the box with their definitions. There is one extra word.

cheap	compete	deaf	distant	draw	effort
frequent	online	prefer	sense	study	wire

1. _____ = unable to hear
2. _____ = try to win or gain something
3. _____ = low-cost, not expensive
4. _____ = know or feel something without seeing or being told about it
5. _____ = a piece of work that is done to answer a research question
6. _____ = like (some person or thing) more than another
7. _____ = attract or pull (someone in a certain direction)
8. _____ = energy or work needed to do something
9. _____ = a long, thin piece of metal, often used to carry electricity
10. _____ = happening often
11. _____ = far away

B Complete the sentences below.

actually	allow	entire	in addition to	in order to	in other words
in touch	notice	partly	smoothly	straight	through

1. I keep _____ with her by phone.
2. She said, "Hi," but he didn't _____. He walked on by.
3. He finds it hard to meet new people and talk to them. _____, he's shy.
4. I had to take two buses _____ get there.
5. Somehow he manages to do a weekend job _____ his regular job.

6. He got the job _____ his own efforts, not because of family connections.

7. We had no problems with the training. Everything went very _____.

8. She looks younger than her husband does, but she's _____ older than he is.

9. You seemed only _____ awake when you answered the phone this morning.

10. The shortest distance between two points is a _____ line.

11. She will not _____ her children to stay up late on school nights.

12. My _____ family—all twenty of us—got together for the holidays.

EXPANDING VOCABULARY

	Nouns	Verbs	Adjectives
1.	attraction	attract	attractive
2.			
3.			
4.			
5.			

A Complete the chart of word families with words from the sentences below.

1. a. Flowers attract certain insects, like bees.
   b. She is an attractive young woman.
   c. It was easy to see the attraction between Jack and Diana.

2. a. His bad behavior often got him into trouble.
   b. Parents teach their children how to behave.

3. a. Do boys and girls go to separate schools in your country?
   b. Separate the light-colored clothes from the dark ones before washing them.
   c. They were married for five years before their separation.

4. **a.** We warned them to be careful after dark.

   b. There is a warning on every cigarette package.

5. **a.** She is too shy to talk to the boys in her class.

   b. His shyness keeps him from going to parties.

B *Gain, sense, shout,* and *waste* **can be nouns or verbs. Use each word as a noun to complete one of the following sentences. Then use it as a verb in a new sentence.**

1. **a.** We didn't do anything useful at the meeting. It was a _____ of time.

   b. _____

   _____

2. **a.** You can be proud of the _____s you have made in learning English.

   b. _____

   _____

3. **a.** I heard a _____, so I turned around to look.

   b. _____

   _____

4. **a.** I don't have a very good _____ of smell.

   b. _____

   _____

PLAYING WITH WORDS

Complete the sentences with words you studied in Chapters 9–12. Write the words in the puzzle.

Across

1. Before you leave the plane, check for your p<u>ersonal</u>_____ belongings.

4. The child's parents warned her not to talk to s_____.

10. You can trust him. He's a man of good c_____.

11. I have socks in v_____ colors.

12. She is a leader in her c_____. Everyone in town respects her.

13. Let's leave early and a_____ the traffic.

Down

2. Our TV uses e_____.

3. He said to call tomorrow. He didn't give a s_____ time.

5. I have a good r_____ with my brother. He's my best friend.

6. A supermarket has a wide v_____ of products.

7. He does exercises to gain s_____.

8. After the rain, the g_____ was very wet.

9. They have busy s_____ lives on weekends. They're always out with friends.

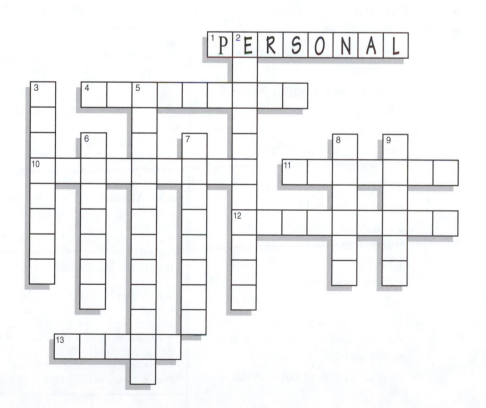

BUILDING DICTIONARY SKILLS

 Look at these dictionary entries.

---

ex·press¹ /ɪkˈsprɛs/ *v* [T] **1** to use words or actions in order to let people know what you are thinking or feeling: *A number of people expressed the fear that they would never get another job.* | *It's hard sometimes for children to* **express themselves**. **2** **express an interest in something** to say that you are interested in something: *She expressed an interest in seeing the old map.*

express² *adj* **1** specific, deliberate, or exact: *It was her* **express wish** *that you inherit her house.* **2** **express train/bus** a train or bus that travels quickly and does not stop in many places

---

Do you see **express**¹ and **express**²? The small raised numbers ¹ and ² are superscripts. They tell you that *express* can be more than one part of speech. One entry for *express* explains the meanings of the verb; the other explains the adjective.

Which meaning of *express* is used in each sentence? Circle *express*¹ or *express*².

1. Is there an express bus this afternoon?   (express¹/express²)

2. She doesn't often express her opinions.   (express¹/express²)

 Words often have more than one meaning. Dictionaries number the meanings.

Look at this entry for *regular*. Write the number of the meaning used in each sentence below.

__4__ 1. He is a regular user of the Internet.

_____ 2. I don't work regular hours. They're always changing.

_____ 3. *Talk* and *look* are regular verbs; *go* and *have* are irregular.

_____ 4. The patient's breathing was slow and regular.

_____ 5. I'll have a regular orange juice—no, wait, a large one, please.

_____ 6. I didn't see my regular dentist because he's away.

_____ 7. He's a famous actor, but he's easy to talk to. He seems like a regular guy.

_____ 8. She has nice, regular teeth.

---

reg·u·lar¹ /ˈrɛgyələ/ *adj*
1 ▸ **REPEATED** ◂ repeated, with the same amount of time or space between each thing and the next: *His heartbeat is strong and regular.* | *Planes were taking off* **at regular intervals**.
2 ▸ **NORMAL SIZE** ◂ of standard size: *fries and a regular coke*
3 ▸ **SAME TIME** ◂ happening or planned for the same time every day, month, year etc.: *regular meetings* | *Once I start working regular hours, things should get better.*
4 ▸ **HAPPENING OFTEN** ◂ happening or doing something very often: *He's one of our regular customers.*
5 ▸ **USUAL** ◂ normal or usual: *She's not our regular babysitter.*
6 ▸ **ORDINARY** ◂ ordinary: *I'm just a regular doctor, not a specialist.*
7 ▸ **EVENLY SHAPED** ◂ evenly shaped with parts or sides of equal size: *regular features* (= an evenly shaped face)
8 ▸ **GRAMMAR** ◂ TECHNICAL a regular verb or noun changes its forms in the same way as most verbs or nouns. The verb "walk" is regular, but "be" is not: **–regularity** /ˌrɛgyəˈlærəti/ *n* [U]

Vocabulary Self-Test 1

**Circle the letter of the word or phrase that best completes each sentence.
Example:**

I like working for her. She is a good _____.

a. software   c. boss

b. needle   d. speech

1. Listen to this singer—she has a beautiful _____.

   a. oil   c. leather

   b. ground   d. voice

2. Please, pay _____ to your driving.

   a. agreement   c. professor

   b. attention   d. medicine

3. Changes in class size will _____ all students and teachers.

   a. cause   c. record

   b. disappear   d. affect

4. The cost of some hotel rooms _____ breakfast.

   a. invents   c. includes

   b. competes   d. develops

5. I thought her name was Joan, but it is _____ JoAnne.

   a. partly   c. by accident

   b. right away   d. actually

6. She has a big _____ on her little sister.

   a. stage   c. research

   b. point   d. influence

7. I don't know all the _____ of the plan.

   a. details   c. wires

   b. insects   d. scores

8. After college, they will _____ for jobs.

   a. imagine   c. decrease

   b. apply   d. warn

9. Before you start your new job, you will need some _____.

    a. forest   **c.** training

    b. bomb   **d.** field

10. I read only part of the report, not the _____ thing.

    a. weak   **c.** distant

    b. gentle   **d.** entire

11. We couldn't find two seats together on the train, so we sat in _____ places.

    a. still   **c.** separate

    b. medical   **d.** daily

12. The two brothers spend a lot of time together. They have a close _____.

    a. laughter   **c.** case

    b. movement   **d.** relationship

13. People usually drive faster on _____ roads.

    a. social   **c.** male

    b. straight   **d.** immediate

14. I didn't _____ myself well. Let me try to explain my idea again.

    a. express   **c.** gain

    b. draw   **d.** create

15. We gain _____ when we eat too much.

    a. points   **c.** sickness

    b. weight   **d.** skills

16. I drove slowly, trying to _____ the bad places in the road.

    a. avoid   **c.** get into

    b. increase   **d.** support

17. The _____ of all the grades in the class was 85%.

    a. study   **c.** closet

    b. average   **d.** report

18. Most stores close at 9:00, but _____ ones stay open later.

    a. certain   **c.** calm

    b. shy   **d.** upset

19. He likes doing things _____, like bicycling and fishing.

   a. outdoors   **c.** anymore

   b. however   **d.** whenever

20. We _____ for the information online, but we couldn't find it.

   a. searched   **c.** referred

   b. wasted   **d.** meant

21. The store will be closed for a short _____—a week at most.

   a. behavior   **c.** supply

   b. period   **d.** rate

22. There were no tables _____ at the first restaurant, so we went to another.

   a. relaxed   **c.** disappointed

   b. available   **d.** creative

23. Let's make an _____ to be there early.

   a. effort   **c.** activity

   b. electricity   **d.** amount

24. It's 11:00? Oh, no! I didn't _____ that it was so late.

   a. contain   **c.** claim

   b. store   **d.** realize

25. The letter from the school _____ classes that the student had missed.

   a. sensed   **c.** concerned

   b. fed   **d.** preferred

26. We expect rain across the whole _____ tomorrow.

   a. set   **c.** region

   b. culture   **d.** explanation

27. Her _____ show clearly on her face.

   a. notes   **c.** emotions

   b. tools   **d.** strangers

28. I'm not shopping for anything _____. I'm looking at all kinds of things.

   a. specific   **c.** somehow

   b. advanced   **d.** ahead

29. The bus makes _____ stops, so it takes a long time to get there.

    a. active   **c.** frequent

    b. low   **d.** sharp

30. They had a long _____ of meetings to plan for the new school.

    a. goal   **c.** character

    b. series   **d.** direction

31. The hospital won't _____ visitors to stay after 9:00 P.M.

    a. practice   **c.** shout

    b. pronounce   **d.** allow

32. He had enough money for only a pair of _____ shoes.

    a. personal   **c.** awake

    b. alike   **d.** cheap

33. The _____ of his letter was to tell us of the change in plans.

    a. purpose   **c.** variety

    b. connection   **d.** season

34. The clothes in the store window _____ a lot of attention.

    a. divided   **c.** pressed

    b. attracted   **d.** noticed

35. I just moved here, so I don't yet know many members of the _____.

    a. discovery   **c.** community

    b. invitation   **d.** strength

36. We said good-bye and promised to keep _____ with each other.

    a. in fact   **c.** in touch

    b. in general   **d.** on the other hand

See the Answer Key on page 239.

UNIT 4

INTO THE WORLD OF BUSINESS

CHAPTER 13

A Family Business

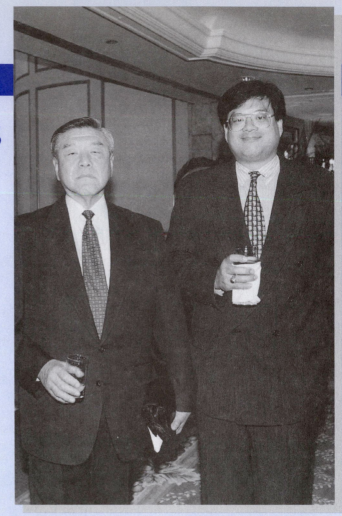

Bruce Yang with his father

GETTING READY TO READ

Answer the question below. Then talk in a small group about the reasons for your answers.

Which of the following sounds best to you? Number your choices from 1 (the best) to 5.

_____ **a.** start my own business

_____ **b.** start a business with a partner or partners

_____ **c.** join a business owned by someone in my family

_____ **d.** go to work for a small local company

_____ **e.** go to work for a large international company

READING

Look at the words and picture next to the reading. Then read without stopping. Don't worry about new words. Don't stop to use a dictionary. Just keep reading!

A Family Business

1   Bruce Yang is a **director** of Taipan Supplies Limited. It is a family business, started by his grandfather. The company has its offices in Taiwan and Hong Kong. The author interviewed Bruce Yang in November of 2002.

2 *Interviewer:* Mr. Yang, what kind of business is Taipan Supplies?

3 *Bruce Yang:* Our company **deals in** three different types of business activity. First, we represent[1] **foreign** companies here in Taiwan. These companies want to sell their **goods** or **services** here, but they don't want to **set up** offices, find people to work for them, and so on. So our company **does business** for them. For example, we've represented some American airlines and companies that make earth-moving equipment.[2]

4   Second, we act as business consultants.[3] We have a lot of experience in construction[4] and in shipping—sending goods by air or sea. So companies sometimes want our advice on these **industries**. They come to us for information about doing business in Taiwan. We also work with Taiwanese companies who want to do business in other countries. And third, we put money into our own projects. For example, right now we have **investments** in a software **firm**, in oil, and in various other things.

5 *Interviewer:* How did your company get started?

6 *Bruce Yang:* My grandfather and his partners set it up back in the 1950s. At first, the company dealt in international **trade**, mostly between Taiwan and the U.S. Then in the '60s, my father joined the firm. He helped it grow in new directions.

continued

[1] *represent* = speak or do things for a person or group who can't be there

[2] A bulldozer is one kind of *earth-moving equipment*

[3] a *consultant* = someone with experience in a specific area whose job is to give advice

[4] *construction* = the building of large things, such as houses, roads, and bridges

7 *Interviewer:* And when did you join the business?

8 *Bruce Yang:* In 1985. At that time, I was working for a bank in Hong Kong. Now I **look after** the financial[5] health of Taipan Supplies.

[5] *financial* = concerned with money or money management

9 *Interviewer:* What's the best thing about working in your family business?

10 *Bruce Yang:* The best thing is to have the chance to work with my father. In my school years, my father was so busy working, I never had a chance to **get to know** him. In working with him in the company, I got to know him as a person, not just as my dad.

11 *Interviewer:* And what's the hardest part of working for your family business?

12 *Bruce Yang:* Working with my father! We are very different in character. We see the world differently. This means our discussions about business can be, shall I say, spirited![6] However, my father is the boss. After discussion and after a decision is made, I work to support that decision.

[6] *spirited* = full of energy and strong feeling

13 *Interviewer:* Do you think your children will follow you into the business?

14 *Bruce Yang:* My children—and my **nieces** and **nephews**— may not have the chance to. The company is doing very well, but the business world is changing at a great rate. So our future is **uncertain**.

Quick Comprehension Check

Read these sentences. Circle T (true) or F (false).

1. Bruce Yang started his own company.	T	F
2. Taipan Supplies Limited is a family business in Japan.	T	F
3. The company has more than one kind of business activity.	T	F
4. Bruce Yang enjoys working with his father.	T	F
5. He and his father think very much alike.	T	F
6. Bruce Yang expects his children to continue the family business.	T	F

EXPLORING VOCABULARY

Thinking about the Vocabulary

Which target words and phrases are new to you? Circle them here and in the reading. Then read "A Family Business" again. Look at the context of each new word and phrase. Can you guess the meaning?

Target Words and Phrases			
director (1)	services (3)	investments (4)	get to know (10)
deals in (3)	set up (3)	firm (4)	nieces (14)
foreign (3)	does business (3)	trade (6)	nephews (14)
goods (3)	industries (4)	look after (8)	uncertain (14)

Using the Vocabulary

 These sentences are **about the reading.** Complete them with the words and phrases in the box.

deals in	foreign	goods	industry	investments
look after	service	set up	trade	uncertain

1. Bruce Yang's company is active in three types of business. The firm _____ these three areas.

2. Bruce's firm works with companies from other countries. These are _____ companies.

3. Some companies make or sell a product you can touch. These products are sometimes called "_____." (This noun is always plural.)

4. Other companies do certain kinds of work for people. They sell a _____, such as cleaning things or giving medical advice.

5. When you start a business, you may have to _____ an office. This means you get an office ready to open.

6. Bruce's company gives advice based on its experience with certain areas of business activity. One of these areas is the construction _____.

7. The company puts money into projects in order to get more money back in the future. This is called making _____.

8. In the 1950s, the company dealt in international _____ —that is, the buying and selling of products between countries.

9. Bruce is in charge of the company's money. It is his job to
_____ the company's "financial health."

10. He cannot be sure what will happen to the company. Its future is

_____.

B These sentences use the target words and phrases **in new contexts.**
Complete them with the words and phrases in the box.

deal in	foreign	goods	industry	investments
looks after	services	set up	trade	uncertain

1. Hollywood is important in the film _____. The American
movie business was born there.

2. He made some smart _____, and they have made him rich.

3. Every student in the school has to study a _____ language.

4. Katya is their baby-sitter. She _____ the children while their
parents are out.

5. The store sells men's clothing only. They don't _____ clothes
for women or children.

6. A fire destroyed all the _____ in the store.

7. Our travel plans are _____ at this point. We're not sure when
we're leaving or where we're going.

8. Most of Mexico's international _____ depends on selling
products to the United States and buying U.S. goods.

9. An increase in the cost of oil led to an increase in the cost of many goods
and _____.

10. Last year, the government _____ a new program to help
workers who lose their jobs.

C Read these sentences. Write the **boldfaced** target words or phrases next to
their definitions.

a. I see my **niece** and **nephew** when I visit my sister and brother-in-law.

b. I met her in college, but I didn't **get to know** her very well.

c. He's a film **director**. In other words, he makes movies.

d. Both banks **do business** with local farmers.

e. She is a lawyer in a large law **firm**.

Target Words/Phrases	Definitions

1. _____*niece*_____ = the daughter of someone's brother or sister

2. _____ = the son of someone's brother or sister

3. _____ = a business with two or more partners

4. _____ = gain an understanding of (a person or place)

5. _____ = a person who leads, controls, or manages a company or activity

6. _____ = be active in the making, buying, and selling of goods and services

Building on the Vocabulary

Studying Collocations

The verb *do* often goes with **business,** as in *The bank doesn't do business on Sundays.* Other useful phrases with *business* are:

- *go into business,* meaning "set up a company and start work"
- *go out of business,* meaning "stop working as a company"
- *on business,* meaning "for business purposes"
- *run a business,* meaning "be in charge of and control a business"

A Complete the sentences with words from the box.

do business	on business	run the business
went into business	went out of business	

1. Are you going to London _____ or for the fun of it?

2. After college, he _____ with his father.

3. The company lost a lot of money and finally _____.

4. Big oil companies _____ with foreign governments.

5. My grandfather is the president of the company, but my parents really

   _____.

B Write three statements using phrases with *business.*

1. _____

2. _____

3. _____

DEVELOPING YOUR SKILLS

Understanding Cause and Effect

Complete the following sentences with *because* using information from "A Family Business." Try not to copy sentences from the reading. Use your own words.

1. Foreign companies sometimes ask Bruce Yang's company to represent them in Taiwan because _____.

2. Companies sometimes come to Taipan Supplies Limited for advice because

   _____.

3. Bruce likes working with his father because _____

   _____.

4. It is hard for Bruce to work with his father because _____

   _____.

5. Bruce doesn't know if his children will follow him into the family business

   because _____.

Summarizing

 Use information from "A Family Business" to complete these notes about Taipan Supplies Limited. Write your additions in the chart.

Dates	Notes
1950s	Bruce Yang's grandfather & his partners set up the company to deal in international trade (U.S. & Taiwan)
1960s	
1985	
today	offices in Taiwan & Hong Kong the company deals in 3 areas: 1. 2. 3.

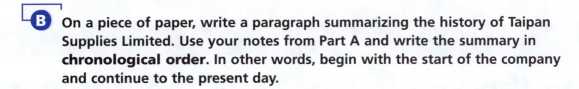

B On a piece of paper, write a paragraph summarizing the history of Taipan Supplies Limited. Use your notes from Part A and write the summary in **chronological order**. In other words, begin with the start of the company and continue to the present day.

Discussion

Talk with a partner about the questions below.

1. Some companies produce goods (they make things) and others deal in services (they do things). Where do the following belong in the chart?

   books, cars, cleaning, computers, education, job training, medical care, oil

Goods	Services
books	

2. What are two more examples you can add to each column?
3. How would you describe Bruce Yang's relationship with his father? Would you like to work for your father or mother? Tell why or why not.

Using New Words

Work with a partner. Take turns completing these statements. Then tell the class something about your partner.

1. I have _____ **niece(s)** and _____ **nephew(s)**.
2. I would like to **get to know** . . .
3. If I were a movie **director**, I would . . .
4. _____ asked me to **look after** . . .
5. I feel **uncertain** about . . .

Writing

Choose a topic. Write a paragraph.

1. How would you feel about being in business with members of your family? Explain.
2. No one can see into the future, but we can imagine the directions our lives may go in. Think about yourself ten years from now. Where do you think you will be? What will you be doing?

CHAPTER 14

When the Employees Own the Company

Jeffrey Hamelman, head baker and worker-owner, shows off bread made with King Arthur flour.

Talk with a partner or in a small group.

1. Have you ever been the boss at work? Would you like a job where you were the boss? Explain why you would or would not.

2. Who works harder, the boss or the people who work for him or her? Tell how you would complete this statement and explain why:

   When you are the boss,

   a. you don't have to work so hard.

   b. you have to work harder.

READING

Look at the words and picture next to the reading. Then read without stopping.

When the Employees Own the Company

1   King Arthur Flour is the oldest **flour** company in the United States. Its flour is of very high **quality**. Just ask the people who **bake** with it. All across North America, people who care about making fine bread buy King Arthur flour. The company even has **customers** in Switzerland, Japan, China, and Saudi Arabia.

2   King Arthur Flour began in 1790 as the Sands, Taylor and Wood Company, and the Sands family has stayed with it all these years. Frank Sands started working there in 1963, when his father was in charge, and later his wife, Brinna, joined him there. Now Frank is the fifth member of the Sands family to lead the company. He will also be the last.

3   A few years ago, Frank and Brinna decided to retire.[1] However, **none** of their children wanted to **take over** the family business, which meant that the future of King Arthur was uncertain. Then one evening, Brinna asked Frank, "Who **besides** our kids is most like family?" The answer was clear: the people who worked at the company. Frank and Brinna trusted them to continue the family tradition. So, in 1996, they began to let the **employees** take over the business. Today, the 160 employees of King Arthur own and run the company.

4   Worker-owned businesses do not all start the same way. In some cases, a group of workers at a successful company find a way to buy it. In other cases, a company fails, but the employees start it up again. Often, a group of people decide to create a new business together. What makes them want to do this? Some want to be part of the decision making at their workplace. Others want a greater chance to share in a company's success. They know that when a company makes money, the owners do, too.

5   There are various types of worker-owned businesses. Some of them make a product, like flour, and others **provide** a service, such as cleaning or health care. There are various ways to **organize** worker-owned businesses, too. However, these businesses usually share certain ideas. One idea is that all the workers—not just the people in charge—should have the chance to be owners. Another is that the worker-owners

[1] *retire* = stop working at the end of a career (usually because of old age)

continued

should have the **right** to vote on business decisions. Then they have real control.

6   Here are the stories of how two more **such** companies began:

- Eight employees at a photocopy shop[2] in Massachusetts (United States) were unhappy with their jobs. "Working **conditions** were terrible and the pay was low," says Stephen Roy, one of the eight. "Plus,[3] we had no job **security**—the manager could **get rid of** any one of us at any time for any reason. We ran the shop for the owners, and we started to ask, 'Why can't we do it for ourselves?'" So they went into business together and started Collective Copies. Twenty years later, they have two shops. One afternoon a month, they close their doors to meet and make business decisions.

- In Coamo, Puerto Rico, there were not many jobs for young people. Miriam Rodriguez, who lived in Coamo, wanted to do something about it. She organized a committee[4] to work on the problem, and the result of their efforts was a furniture business, Las Flores Metalarte. The business now has 180 worker-owners producing tables, chairs, kitchen cabinets,[5] and so on. The success of the company has led to other new businesses in the town, including a sandwich shop and a child care center.

7   According to a study in Italy, worker-owned businesses are good for their communities. They lead to a higher quality of life. The researchers who did the study looked at things like health care, education, and social activities in many Italian towns. They also considered problems in the towns, such as **crime**. They found that towns with more worker-owned businesses were better places to live in almost every way.

Brinna Sands's words come from an article by Per Ola and Emily D'Aulaire, "Baking Up a Business," *Smithsonian* (November 2000): 114–115.

[2] a *photocopy shop* = a business that uses machines to make copies of print materials

[3] *plus* = and also

[4] a *committee* = a group of people asked to do a certain job, make decisions, etc.

[5] kitchen *cabinets*

Quick Comprehension Check

Read these sentences. Circle T (true) or F (false).

1. King Arthur Flour was a family business for many years.   T   F

2. All worker-owned companies start out as family businesses.   T   F

3. The workers at King Arthur bought the company after it failed. T   F

4. Worker-owned businesses are not all the same.   T   F

5. Workers gain more control when they become worker-owners.   T   F

6. There are worker-owned businesses only in the United States.   T   F

EXPLORING VOCABULARY

Thinking about the Vocabulary

Which target words and phrases are new to you? Circle them here and in the reading. Then read "When the Employees Own the Company" again. Look at the context of each new word and phrase. Can you guess the meaning?

Target Words and Phrases			
flour (1)	none (3)	provide (5)	conditions (6)
quality (1)	take over (3)	organize (5)	security (6)
bake (1)	besides (3)	right (5)	get rid of (6)
customers (1)	employees (3)	such (6)	crime (7)

Using the Vocabulary

 These sentences are about the reading. What is the meaning of each **boldfaced** word or phrase? Circle a, b, or c.

1. King Arthur Flour has over a million **customers**. *Customers* means:

   a. people who run a business   b. people who buy goods or services   c. people who sell a product

2. Frank and Brinna Sands hoped one of their children would continue the family business, but **none** of them wanted to. *None* means:

   a. all   b. most   c. not any

3. Frank and Brinna were ready to give up control of King Arthur. But their children didn't want to **take over** the company. *Take over* means:

   a. take control of   b. compete with   c. realize

4. Brinna asked who **besides** their children were most important to them. *Besides* means:

   a. because of   b. in addition to   c. in order to

5. Some businesses produce goods and others **provide** services. *Provide* means:

   a. avoid   b. waste   c. supply

6. There are various ways to **organize** and run a worker-owned business. *Organize* means:

   a. plan or set up   b. destroy   c. avoid

7. There are many worker-owned businesses in the world. The reading describes three **such** companies. *Such* means:

   a. of the kind just described
   b. on a regular basis
   c. in addition

8. The copy shop workers worried that their boss could **get rid of** them easily. *Get rid of* someone means:

   a. make someone leave
   b. increase someone's pay
   c. look after someone

9. According to a study in Italy, there is less **crime** in towns with many worker-owned businesses. *Crime* means:

   a. fun social activities
   b. actions that are against the law
   c. relationships among people

B These sentences use the target words and phrases **in new contexts.** Complete them with the words and phrases in the box.

besides	crime	customers	get rid of	none
organized	provide	such	take over	

1. The store went out of business because it didn't have enough _____.

2. There were three pay phones on the wall, but _____ of them worked.

3. _____ taking four courses, she is working 20 hours a week.

4. While the teacher is out sick, someone else will _____ the class.

5. I'm sure he can _____ an explanation for what he did.

6. People in the city are upset about the high _____ rate.

7. Al has to write a 20-page paper. He has never written _____ a long paper.

8. Beatriz _____ the class party. She knows who is bringing what food, who is in charge of the music, and all the other details.

9. The neighbors' dog keeps coming into our yard. We don't want him around, but we don't know how to _____ him.

Read each definition and look at the paragraph number in parentheses ( ).
Look back at the reading to **find the target word** for each definition. Write
it in the chart.

Definition	Target Word
1. a powder made from wheat[1] or another grain, used for making bread, cakes, etc. (1)	
2. how good something is, its character (1)	
3. cook food inside an oven[2] (1)	
4. the people who work for a person or business (3)	
5. something that a person is allowed to do by law (5)	
6. all the things that affect the place someone lives or works (6)	
7. safety from having to change or from losing something (6)	

[1]*wheat*

[2]bread in an *oven*

Building on the Vocabulary

Studying Word Grammar

Remember: A **suffix** is a letter or letters added to the end of a word to make a
new word. Look at the words and suffixes in the word family for *employ* ("give a
job to"):

> *employ**er*** = a person who gives a job to someone
>
> *employ**ee*** = a person who works for another person, for a company, etc.
>
> *employ**ment*** = work; the fact or condition of having a job
>
> ***un**employ**ment*** = the opposite of *employment* (The prefix *un-* means "not" or
> "the opposite of.")

A Complete the paragraph with the five words from the word family for *employ*.

The hospital is the biggest _____ in the community. It
₍₁₎

has over 800 _____ s. It _____ s doctors,
₍₂₎ ₍₃₎

nurses, office workers, cooks, and so on. Of course, the hospital is not the only

place to find _____ in town. There are many jobs available in
₍₄₎

the area right now, so the _____ rate is low.
₍₅₎

B The **boldfaced** words have the suffixes *-er* and *-ee.* Can you guess their
meanings? Write the words next to their definitions.

a. He's a racehorse **trainer**.

b. On the first day at my new job, I met the other **trainees**.

1. _____ = a person who teaches skills, especially for a job or sport

2. _____ = people who are receiving training.

DEVELOPING YOUR SKILLS

Understanding Main Ideas and Supporting Details

**Supply a detail from the reading to support each of the general
statements below. Use your own words and write complete sentences.**

1. Sometimes the employees of a company take it over. <u>For example, this</u>
   <u>happened at King Arthur Flour when Frank and Brinna Sands retired.</u>

2. Sometimes a group of employees work to create a business together. _____
   _____
   _____

3. Some worker-owned companies produce goods to sell. _____
   _____
   _____

4. Worker-owned businesses can have a good effect on their communities.
   _____
   _____

Summarizing

Do the following tasks on a piece of paper. Use information from the reading, but try not to copy sentences from the reading.

1. Summarize the history of King Arthur Flour, from 1790 to the present.
2. Describe the way Collective Copies began.
3. Describe Las Flores Metalarte.

Sharing Opinions

Talk about these questions in a small group.

1. The employees at a worker-owned business own a share of their company. How do you think this affects how they feel about their jobs? How do you think it affects the way they do their jobs?
2. The reading says, "According to a study in Italy, worker-owned businesses are good for their communities." How do you think such businesses help their communities?

Using New Words

Work with a partner. Choose five target words or phrases from the list on page 131. On a piece of paper, use each word or phrase in a sentence.

Writing

Choose a topic. Write a paragraph.

1. The phrase *working conditions* refers to all the things about your job that affect how you feel about it. They can include everything from the air quality in your workplace to your sense of job security. Imagine a job with great working conditions and describe it.
2. Are you good or bad at organizing things? Write about organizing something in your life—for example, your closet, your time on weekends, a party, or a trip.

CHAPTER 15

She Finally Did It

Elizabeth (Betty) Nice Weber presenting a check

GETTING READY TO READ

Talk with a partner or in a small group.

1. Would you like to be a millionaire?[1] Check (✓) your answer:

   ❑ Yes   ❑ No   ❑ Maybe

2. How do you think most millionaires get rich?

3. If you become very rich, what will you do with your money?

[1] a *millionaire* = a person with $1,000,000 or more

READING

Look at the words and definitions next to the reading. Then read without stopping.

She Finally Did It

1   While Betty Nice was growing up, her family did not have much money. They **could not afford** to buy a house, and the apartment they **rented** was in a bad part of town. Betty knew she wanted something better. She dreamed of living another kind of life, but how would she make it happen? She did not know. In fact, she had no idea what she wanted to do when she grew up. "All I knew," she says, "was I wanted to be a millionaire."

2   After high school, Betty went to college to study business. She took courses at four colleges, and although she came close, she never managed to get her **degree**. She says now, "I wasn't cut out for[1] the classroom."

[1] *not be cut out for = not have the right qualities for (a certain job or activity)*

3   Betty then went to work as a **secretary**. She spent years working for a law firm, doing all the usual office work. The job was nothing special, and she did not **earn** a lot. She and her husband could not save any money. With no savings in the bank, she had no sense of security. Betty wanted more.

4   During this period, she also had a series of part-time jobs in **sales**, sometimes going door-to-door, and sometimes organizing parties in the evening to sell things to friends and neighbors. In 11 years, she worked for nine different companies and sold lots and lots of different things. Brushes, **jewelry**, and skin care products were just a few. "I tried everything!" she says with a laugh. Betty made some money, but not much. She says, "It **wasn't worth** the hours I was putting in."[2] She did not know what to do. "I worked so hard, and I failed at everything. My husband paid the bills and supported me through it all." But all the time that Betty was "failing," she was learning. She was gaining business skills and becoming a better salesperson.

[2] *putting in = giving or spending (time)*

5   Betty was almost ready to give up when she heard about another company. It sounded different, so she **looked into** it and found out more about it. Then, after **thinking over**

continued

what she had learned, she decided to take a chance. She gave up her job at the law firm after 18 years as a secretary and became a full-time salesperson. She went on to sell everything from motor oil for cars to burglar alarms[3] for houses to **pills** for people trying to lose weight. She also recruited[4] other salespeople, and she became an **officer** in the company. After four years, Betty was a millionaire. Soon she was making over a million dollars a year!

6   At age 44, Betty was living a dream come true. She could afford **whatever** she wanted. She and her husband bought a **huge** house (it has 11 bathrooms), and they took their children on exciting trips all over the world. At that point Betty had everything she had ever hoped for. So, what does a person do when she has everything? Betty decided, "Now it's my **turn** to give."

7   Betty set up the Weber Foundation of Helping Hands. "There are a lot of families out there in need," she says, thinking especially of parents with very sick children. She wanted to help not only her own family but also people she did not know. Today, the Weber Foundation does that. In its first 18 months, it **gave away** more than $100,000. For Betty, it is another dream come true.

Betty Nice Weber's words come from Eileen McNamara, "Now a Boss but Still Nice," *Boston Globe,* October 15, 2000, B: 1, and from Phil Santoro, "Sharing Her Success," *Boston Globe,* March 3, 2002, North Weekly section: 9.

[3] *burglar alarms* = machines that warn people (by making a loud noise, for example) when someone enters a building

[4] *recruit* = find new people to work in a company, join an organization, etc.

Quick Comprehension Check

Read these sentences. Circle T (true) or F (false).

1. Betty Nice grew up poor.   T   F

2. She graduated from college with a business degree.   T   F

3. She worked for many years as a secretary.   T   F

4. Working at a law firm made her rich.   T   F

5. Betty doesn't care about money.   T   F

6. She gives away money to families who need it.   T   F

EXPLORING VOCABULARY

Thinking about the Vocabulary

Which target words and phrases are new to you? Circle them here and in the reading. Then read "She Finally Did It" again. Look at the context of each new word and phrase. Can you guess the meaning?

Target Words and Phrases			
could not afford (1)	**earn** (3)	**looked into** (5)	**whatever** (6)
rented (1)	**sales** (4)	**thinking over** (5)	**huge** (6)
degree (2)	**jewelry** (4)	**pills** (5)	**turn** (6)
secretary (3)	**wasn't worth** (4)	**officer** (5)	**gave away** (7)

Using the Vocabulary

 Complete these sentences. Write *jewelry, a pill,* and *a secretary.*

1. He's taking _____.

2. She's wearing _____.

3. She's _____.

B These sentences are **about the reading**. Complete them with the words and phrases in the box.

couldn't afford	degree	earn	gives away	huge
looked into	officer	rented	sales	thought it over
turn	wasn't worth	whatever		

1. Betty's family _____ a house. They didn't have enough money to buy one.

2. They didn't own their apartment. They _____ it from the owner.

3. Betty didn't finish her college studies, so she didn't get a _____.

4. She wasn't paid a lot at the law firm. She didn't _____ much money.

5. Betty also worked part-time in _____. She sold various products.

6. The money she got from selling things was not enough for all the hours she spent selling them. The money _____ the time.

7. She heard something about a company and she wanted more information, so she read about it and asked questions. She _____ it.

8. She took time to think carefully about joining the company. She _____.

9. Betty showed a lot of ability, so the company made her an _____, one of the people in charge.

10. Now she has money for anything she wants. She can afford _____ she wants.

11. Betty's house has many, many rooms. It is _____.

12. After Betty became rich, she decided it was her _____ to give. It was the right time for her to do something for others.

13. The Weber Foundation of Helping Hands _____ money to people in need. People who receive the money don't have to do anything for it, and they don't have to give it back.

These sentences use the target words and phrases **in new contexts**.
Complete them with the words and phrases in the box.

can afford	degree	earned	gave it away	huge
is worth	looked into it	officers	rented	sales
think it over	turn	whatever		

1. You have the right to say _____ you want.

2. He received his _____ from the University of Toronto.

3. They make a lot of money, so they _____ to eat in restaurants whenever they want.

4. In a company, the army, or the police, the _____ are the people who make decisions and give orders.

5. That's not cheap jewelry! It _____ thousands of dollars.

6. A career in _____ would be hard for a shy person.

7. They didn't take the train to Madrid. They _____ a car and drove.

8. The bus driver worked extra hours, so she _____ more money than usual.

9. You washed the dishes last night, so tonight is my _____.

10. I didn't try to sell my old bicycle. I _____.

11. They have invited him to join the firm, but he needs time to _____.

12. Yesterday I heard about an apartment for rent, so I _____ right away.

13. Going into business with my mother was a _____ mistake. We can't agree on anything!

Building on the Vocabulary

Studying Collocations

The adjective *worth* can follow *be* or another linking verb (such as *seem, sound,* or *look*). A thing can be worth:

- an amount of money: *The house is worth a million dollars.*
- time or effort: *Maybe we can fix it—it seems worth a try.*
- doing something: *The service is slow, but the food is worth waiting for.*

Write three statements with the adjective *worth*.

1. _____

2. _____

3. _____

DEVELOPING YOUR SKILLS

Reading Between the Lines

You cannot find the answers to these questions given in the reading. These are inference or opinion questions. To answer them, you must use what you already know in addition to information from the reading.

1. Was money the only thing that mattered to Betty? Explain your answer.

   _____

   _____

   _____

   _____

2. How would you describe Betty's character? Why do you see her this way?

   _____

   _____

   _____

   _____

3. Why do you think Betty didn't stop working after she became a millionaire?

   _____

   _____

   _____

   _____

Summarizing

On a piece of paper, write a summary of "She Finally Did It." Use no more than ten sentences. Include information about:

- Betty's life and dreams as a child
- her early career
- her part-time jobs
- her success as a salesperson
- the Weber Foundation of Helping Hands

Sharing Opinions

Talk about these questions in a small group.

1. Compare your answers to the three questions under **Reading Between the Lines**. In what ways do you agree or disagree?

2. What do you think of these two common sayings: "Money can't buy happiness" and "The best things in life are free"? Do you agree or disagree with these sayings? Why?

3. Why might someone not want to be a millionaire? Describe some reasons.

Using New Words

Work with a partner. Take turns completing these statements. Then tell the class something about your partner.

1. I can't **afford** . . .
2. I have never **rented** . . .
3. I would like to have a **degree** in . . .
4. The movie ". . ." **isn't worth** seeing.
5. A career in **sales** would be . . . for me.

Writing

Choose a topic. Write a paragraph.

1. For some people, success means making a lot of money. Is that true for you? Describe your idea of success.

2. Write a letter to a friend you haven't seen in a long time. Explain to your friend that you are now a millionaire and describe how you became so rich. Invite your friend to visit you.

CHAPTER 16

A Language on the Move

Doing business in English

GETTING READY TO READ

**Answer the three parts of question 1 by circling a number from 1 to 5.
Then talk about your answers to questions 1 and 2 in a small group or
with your class.**

Very ⟵⟶ Not at all

1. In your country:

   a. Are English classes common in the schools?   1   2   3   4   5

   b. Is English important for many jobs?   1   2   3   4   5

   c. Is English important in the business world?   1   2   3   4   5

2. When, where, and why do businesspeople from your country use English?

Look at the words and definitions next to the reading. Then read without stopping.

A Language on the Move

1   Filiz Yilmaz works for a company in Istanbul and usually speaks Turkish at work. When she travels to England on business, she uses English. But when she goes to Germany or Brazil, she does not use German or Portuguese. She **deals with** people there in English, too. "And I use English in Japan and Thailand," she says. "English is the language of international business."

2   How did English get to be so **popular**? It is not the oldest living language, nor is it the most beautiful to the ear. It includes sounds that are hard to pronounce and many words that are hard to spell. So why has this language **spread** so far?

3   Some people would answer this question by pointing to the influence of music and movies. American films do seem to be everywhere now, but they often **appear** in other languages, and people can enjoy songs in English without understanding the words. So this cannot be the whole explanation.

4   Part of the answer can be found in the character of the language. English has certain **qualities** that make it especially useful. For one thing, its grammar is **quite** simple. It is relatively[1] easy to learn the **rules** of English—what is and is not allowed, or how the language works. For example, learners of English do not have to worry about the gender of a noun (that is, whether it is masculine, feminine, or neuter),[2] **while** learners of many other languages do. In German, for example, *der Mond* (the word for the moon) is masculine but *die Sonne* (the sun) is feminine. You would expect the words *girl* and *woman* (*das Mädchen* and *das Weib*) to be feminine, but they are neuter!

5   English also has a huge vocabulary. Early English developed from Germanic languages, which gave it the most common words we use today, such as *the, is, of, go, you, man,* and *woman.* However, from the beginning, English **borrowed** words from other European languages, including

[1] *relatively* = compared to others

[2] *masculine, feminine,* or *neuter* = male, female, or neither

continued

Latin (*secretary, attract, compete,* and *invent*) and Greek (*alphabet, mathematics,* and *technology*). After invaders[3] from France took over England in the year 1066, English gained a great many French words, such as *officer, foreign, crime,* and *service.* **Since** that time, English has welcomed useful new words from many other languages—from Spanish, Arabic, Turkish, Urdu, Chinese, and Japanese, to name just a few.

6   To understand the spread of English, we also have to look at **political** and economic[4] history. During the 1600s and 1700s, people from England **sailed** all over the world, taking their language to North America, Africa, India, and Australia. New **nations** were born, and their governments used English. In the 1800s, England led the Industrial Revolution: New machines were invented, factories were built, and the city of London became the world's great financial[5] center. That made English the language of money. In the 1900s, it became the language of science and air travel, too. All through the 1900s, the United States grew in power and influence, and the English language grew right along with it.

7   Then came the Internet. As Filiz Yilmaz remembers it, "People at my company realized that the Internet could be quite useful to us. But at first, everything online was in English. It gave us another reason to know this language." Soon people in many countries were going online, both for business and for personal reasons. Some of them used to see English only in the classroom, but now they needed English on a regular basis, whenever they wanted to "surf the Net."[6]

8   Today, there are business schools teaching all their courses in English even in non-English-speaking countries. These schools want their students to have the language skills **necessary** for doing business in international **markets**. Companies around the world are **investing** in English classes for their employees. They believe in English as the language of the future.

9   There are over 300 million native speakers of English (that is, people who speak it as their first language). Many more speak Mandarin Chinese—almost 900 million. But few of them are outside of China, while there are people who know English all over the world. There may be a billion people who speak some variety of English as a second, third, or fourth language. Filiz says, "With so many people using English, I can't imagine any other language taking its place. I think English for business is here to stay."

[3] *invaders* = people who enter and take over a country by force, as with an army

[4] *economic* = referring to money, goods, and services: how they are produced and used

[5] *financial* = relating to money or the management of money

[6] *surf the Net* = look quickly through sites on the Internet for things that interest you

Quick Comprehension Check

Read these sentences. Circle T (true) or F (false).

1. People around the world use English to talk business.   T   F

2. American movies are the biggest reason why English is so   T   F
   popular.

3. Many English words come from other languages.   T   F

4. England was a world power before the United States.   T   F

5. Companies around the world think English is the language   T   F
   of the future.

6. The same numbers of people speak Chinese and English.   T   F

EXPLORING VOCABULARY

Thinking about the Vocabulary

**Which target words and phrases are new to you? Circle them here and in
the reading. Then read "A Language on the Move" again. Look at the
context of each new word and phrase. Can you guess the meaning?**

Target Words and Phrases			
deals with (1)	qualities (4)	borrowed (5)	nations (6)
popular (2)	quite (4)	since (5)	necessary (8)
spread (2)	rules (4)	political (6)	markets (8)
appear (3)	while (4)	sailed (6)	investing (8)

Using the Vocabulary

 These sentences are **about the reading**. Complete them with the words
and phrases in the box.

appear	borrowed	deals with	invests	markets
necessary	political	rules	since	spread

1. Filiz Yilmaz does business with people in several countries. She

   _____ people in Germany, Brazil, Japan, Thailand, and the

   United States.

2. The number of English speakers has grown. The language has

   _____ around the world.

3. American films are usually shown in English, but they _____ in other languages, too.

4. Languages have _____ (for grammar and spelling, for example). These tell us how to use words so that other people can understand us.

5. English has a big vocabulary because it has always _____ words from other languages. It has grown by copying useful foreign words.

6. Beginning in the year 1066, many French words entered the English language. _____ that time—in other words, starting then and continuing to the present—English has continued to add words from other languages.

7. To understand why English has spread over so much of the world, we have to study _____ history. This concerns power, governments, and relationships between countries.

8. Certain language skills are _____ for business. Businesspeople need them.

9. After finishing business school, some people go on to work in international _____, **i.e.,** in areas concerned with buying and selling.

10. When a company _____ in English-language training for its employees, it spends money. It does this because it expects the training to result in more money later.

Common Abbreviations
The abbreviation *i.e.* is short for the Latin words *id est,* meaning "that is." This abbreviation, like the phrase "in other words," is often used to introduce an explanation.

B These sentences use the target words and phrases **in new contexts**. Complete them with the words and phrases in the box.

appeared	borrow	deal with	invested	market
necessary	political	rules	since	spreads

1. The verb _____ means "copy and use" when it refers to words or ideas. It can also mean "take something, use it, and then give it back," like a library book or money from a bank.

2. They _____ their money well and ended up rich.

3. You can't do that—it's against the _____ of the game.

4. News always _____ quickly among the employees.

5. Suddenly, a face _____ at my window. I was so surprised that it made me jump.

6. It is not _____ to wear a jacket and tie, but he can if he wants to.

7. The phrase _____ *science* refers to the study of government.

8. The company has customers in Europe and Asia, but the main _____ for their software is the United States.

9. Elizabeth has looked after her niece and nephew _____ her sister died last year.

10. I won't _____ that company again. They make high-quality goods, but their customer service is terrible.

C Read these sentences. Write the **boldfaced** target words next to their definitions.

a. It is hard to get to know her. She seems **quite** shy.

b. That song was very **popular** last year.

c. Almost 200 countries belong to the United **Nations**.

d. I'd like to **sail** around the Mediterranean Sea.

e. She likes foreign films, **while** her husband prefers Hollywood movies.

f. She has all the **qualities** the boss likes in an employee: She's smart, hard working, and creative.

Target Words	Definitions
1. _____	= countries
2. _____	= more than a little but not extremely
3. _____	= liked, accepted, or used by a lot of people
4. _____	= parts of the character of a person or thing that make that one different from others
5. _____	= but (used to present differences between two facts or ideas)
6. _____	= travel across the water on a boat or ship

Building on the Vocabulary

The word *since* is used to show when an action began. Use *since* + a point in time (for example, a time, a date, or an event). *Since* is usually used in sentences with verbs in the present perfect or present perfect progressive tense: *He has lived here since 1991. I have been waiting since 2:30. She's been avoiding him since the party.*

Complete the statements. Use *since* + a point in time.

Example: I have known my friend <u>Omar since our first day of school.</u>

1. I have studied English _____.

2. I've been using this book _____.

3. I have known my friend _____   _____.
   (name)

4. My family has lived in _____   _____.
   (place)

DEVELOPING YOUR SKILLS

Reading for Details

Read these sentences. Then reread "A Language on the Move" for the answers. If the reading doesn't give the information, check (✓) *It doesn't say*.

	True	False	It doesn't say.
1. Filiz Yilmaz uses English in Japan and Brazil.			
2. English has harder rules than most other languages.			
3. English has the largest vocabulary of any language.			
4. The Industrial Revolution started in England.			
5. English became the language of science in the 1800s.			
6. The Internet started in California.			
7. Some companies pay for their employees to learn English.			
8. More people speak English as their second, third, or fourth language than as their first.			

Understanding Topics of Paragraphs

A Where is the information about these topics in "A Language on the Move"? Scan the reading and write the paragraph number.

__6__ a. political and economic influences

_____ b. numbers of English speakers

_____ c. the effect of the Internet

_____ d. Filiz Yilmaz's use of English

_____ e. the influence of American movies and music

_____ f. how English developed its huge vocabulary

_____ g. English for international markets

B On a piece of paper, write a sentence or two about each topic in Part A, beginning with the topic of the first paragraph and continuing in order. Do not copy sentences from the reading. Use your own words.

Example: Filiz Yilmaz uses English when she travels to other countries on business.

Discussion

Work with a partner and take turns asking the questions below.

1. What English words can you list that sound like words in your first language? Where do you think the words came from?

2. How will knowing English affect your future? How much English do you need to know?

Using New Words

Work with a partner. Choose five target words or phrases from the list on page 147. On a piece of paper, use each word or phrase in a sentence.

Writing

Choose a topic. Write a paragraph.

1. People invest a lot of time and money in learning English, and nobody wants to waste either one. What advice would you give a new learner on how to invest his or her time and money well?

2. When, where, and why did you start to learn English? How did you feel about the experience?

Wrap-up

REVIEWING VOCABULARY

A Think about the meanings of the words in each group below. Cross out the one word that does not belong in each group.

1. nephew   uncle   ~~officer~~   niece
2. secretary   employee   director   quality
3. rules   customers   sales   markets
4. organize   sail   plan   set up
5. invest   earn   bake   borrow

B Match the words and phrases below with their definitions. There are two extra words or phrases.

deal with	foreign	goods	huge	industry	look into
nation	political	rent	think over	uncertain	whatever

1. _____ = very, very big
2. _____ = anything
3. _____ = not known or not sure
4. _____ = concerned with government or power
5. _____ = have a business connection with
6. _____ = things that are produced to be sold
7. _____ = from a country that is not your own
8. _____ = try to find out the facts about something
9. _____ = consider (something) carefully before making a decision
10. _____ = an area of business, usually dealing in the production of something

EXPANDING VOCABULARY

Some verbs are **transitive**. After a transitive verb, there is a direct object, usually a noun or pronoun. For example, the verb *take* is transitive and needs a direct object: *He took **a pill**. / He took **it**.* We cannot say *He took.*

Other verbs are **intransitive**, such as *sleep.* There can be no direct object after the verb *sleep: He slept.*

Some verbs can be used either way—with or without a direct object: *I drove **my car** to the beach* or *I drove to the beach.*

 A Underline the verbs in the sentences below. Circle any direct objects after the verbs. Which verbs are transitive, which are intransitive, and which can be either? Check (✓) your answers in the chart.

	Transitive	Intransitive
1. a. I <u>spread</u> some (butter) on my bread. b. English <u>spread</u> around the world.	✓	✓
2. a. She often bakes on weekends. b. She baked a birthday cake.		
3. a. I'll trade my candy bar for yours. b. We trade with foreign countries.		
4. a. Can you sail a boat? b. The ship sails at 10:00.		
5. a. I can't afford the rent. b. Can they afford a new car?		
6. a. He finally appeared at 9:30. b. Stars appeared in the sky.		

B On a piece of paper, write at least six sentences with at least six different verbs. Use verbs that were target words in Unit 4. Mark each verb *T* for transitive or *I* for intransitive.

             T
Example: <u>Let's organize a class party.</u>

PLAYING WITH WORDS

There are 12 target words from Unit 4 in this puzzle. The words go across (→)and down (↓). Find the words and circle them. Then use them to complete the sentences below.

```
M  C  B  P  R  O  V  I  D  E
B  O  E  R  I  G  H  T  E  S
O  N  S  X  Z  C  V  X  G  E
R  D  I  K  H  R  Z  G  R  C
R  I  D  W  H  I  L  E  E  U
O  T  E  W  X  M  K  Z  E  R
W  I  S  V  Z  E  V  Q  X  I
P  O  P  U  L  A  R  X  K  T
M  N  E  C  E  S  S  A  R  Y
V  S  X  Q  U  A  L  I  T  Y
```

1. Working _____conditions_____ were very bad, so many employees quit.

2. My friends are bringing the food and I'll _____ the drinks.

3. It took him four years to earn his college _____.

4. All patients must sign certain medical forms. They will give you the _____ forms at the hospital.

5. The _____ rate usually goes up during periods of high unemployment.

6. She buys cheap clothes. She can't afford anything of high _____.

7. Job _____ is worth a lot to him. He hates worrying about the future.

8. That color is very _____ this season. Everybody is wearing it.

9. Jack enjoys dealing with the customers, _____ his brother hates it.

10. I often _____ books from the public library.

11. At what age do people get the _____ to vote in your country?

12. She works 15 hours a week _____ going to school full-time.

BUILDING DICTIONARY SKILLS

Regular and Irregular Verb Forms

When a verb is **regular,** your dictionary may show only its **base form** (or **simple form**). Here are two examples:

---

ap·pear /ə'pɪr/ v [I] **1** to begin to be seen: *Suddenly, clouds began to appear in the sky.* | *A face appeared at the window.* **2** to seem: *The man **appeared to be** dead.* | *The noise **appeared to come** from the closet.* **3** to take part in a movie...

---

earn /ɚn/ v [T] **1** to get money by working: *Alan earns $30,000 a year.* **2** to make a profit from business, or from putting money in a bank, lending it etc.: *I **earned** $5000 **from my** investments last year.* **3** to get something that...

To form the simple past tense of a regular verb, add *-ed;* to form participles, add *-ed* (for the past) or *-ing* (for the present).

When a verb is **irregular,** dictionaries usually show the simple past tense form and the participles. Look at this example:

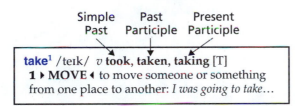

Simple Past Past Participle Present Participle

take[1] /teɪk/ v **took, taken, taking** [T]
1 ▸ MOVE ◂ to move someone or something from one place to another: *I was going to take...*

Complete the sentences below. Write the simple past tense form of *deal, set,* **or** *spread.*

---

deal[2] v **dealt, dealt** /dɛlt/, **dealing 1** [I,T] also **deal out** to give out playing cards to players in a game: *Whose...*

---

set[1] /sɛt/ v **set, set, setting**
1 ▸ RECORD/STANDARD ETC. ◂ [T] to do or decide something that other things...

---

spread[1] /sprɛd/ v **spread, spread, spreading**
1 ▸ OPEN/ARRANGE ◂ [T] also **spread out** to open...

---

1. He _____ the news to all his friends by e-mail.

2. I _____ with a new officer at the bank yesterday.

3. He _____ up a meeting, and everyone agreed to come.

UNIT 5

HEALTH MATTERS

CHAPTER 17

Living to 100 and Beyond

Ponce de Léon on his search for the Fountain of Youth

GETTING READY TO READ

Life expectancy means the number of years a person will probably live. The average life expectancy for a country is how long people in that country usually live. For example, for people in the United States, the average life expectancy is about 77 years. For Canadians, it is almost 80.

Talk with a partner or with your class.

1. What do you think the average life expectancy is for people in your country?

2. In what countries do you think people have the longest life expectancy? And the shortest? Why?

3. Do you think life expectancy is the same for both men and women? Tell why or why not.

READING

Look at the words and pictures next to the reading. Then read without stopping. Don't worry about new words. Don't stop to use a dictionary. Just keep reading!

Living to 100 and Beyond

1   Would you like to live to 100? Many people would. Some have dreamed of living even longer—perhaps **forever**. We know this has long been a popular idea because many cultures have legends[1] about ways to avoid growing old.

2   In Europe in the 1400s, people heard stories about a wonderful spring[2] somewhere in Eastern Asia. Drinking the water from this spring was supposed to make a person young again. It is **likely** that the Spanish explorer[3] Juan Ponce de Léon heard these stories. Maybe they were on his mind when he sailed to the Americas with Columbus. After arriving in Puerto Rico, Ponce de Léon heard about an island with a **similar** spring. So, he decided to look for it, and he invested in three ships. In 1513, he went searching for the island, but he ended up in Florida, never finding the island or the spring that people now call the "Fountain[4] of Youth." When Ponce de Léon died eight years later, he was 61 years old. That may seem young, but it was actually a very long life for a man of his times and his way of life.

3   Not long ago, scientists **generally** agreed that the human body could not **possibly** last more than 120 years. Nobody believes 120 to be the **limit** anymore. People have already lived **beyond** that age. A Japanese man, Shigechiyo Izumi, lived to almost 121, and a woman in France, Jeanne Louise Calment, **made it** to 122. People in many parts of the world are living longer lives now than people did in the past. This is partly because of better public health and safer water supplies. Greater understanding of how to **treat** heart problems has made a big difference **as well**. Scientists are learning more all the time about how we can live longer, healthier lives. Maybe someday they will even invent a pill to stop the aging **process** completely.

continued

[1] a *legend* = a well-known story from an earlier time in history

[2] a *spring* = a place where water comes up naturally from the ground

[3] an *explorer* = someone who travels to learn about unknown places

[4] a *fountain*

4   While you are waiting for that wonderful pill, there are things you can do to increase your life expectancy. You just have to follow these three simple rules:

Rule #1: Treat your body well.

Your everyday **lifestyle** influences how long you will live. For example, smoking can take years off your life. (Even if it doesn't make you sick, smoking will affect your skin and make you look older.) So don't smoke, get enough sleep, and lead an active life. Be sure to eat right, too. In other words, eat the kinds of food that are good for you, and don't eat too much.

*Rule #2: Don't take **risks.***

Forget about motorcycles[5] and take the bus. Wear your seat belt when you travel by car. Also, choose a nice, safe job. Don't go to sea and work on a fishing boat—that's a dangerous way to **make a living**. If Ponce de Léon had followed Rule #2, he might have lived many more years. Instead, he ended up fighting Native Americans in Florida and died of his **injuries**.

Rule #3: Choose your parents carefully.

You say this one is not so simple? That's true. However, about 70% of your life expectancy depends on your genes,[6] and you get your genes from your parents. Genes control your hair and eye color and much, much more. If people in your family usually live long lives, then the chances are good that you will, too.

5   Scientists have already found genes that influence the aging process in fruit flies and in one kind of worm.[7] By changing these genes, they have managed to **double** the time that these flies and worms can live. Of course they are looking for ways to do that for humans as well.

6   Some final advice for anyone who wants to live to 100: It helps to be born in Australia or Japan, and it helps to be born female. Only one in 10,000 people in the United States lives to be 100, but people in Australia and Japan generally do better. The average Australian or Japanese man can expect to see age 77, while his sister can expect to reach 83.

[5] *a motorcycle*

[6] *your genes* = the parts of cells in your body that control qualities you get from your parents

[7] a *worm*

Quick Comprehension Check

Read these sentences. Circle T (true) or F (false).

1. Many cultures have stories from the past about ways to stay young. T F

2. Scientists all agree: Nobody can live past 120. T F

3. The reading gives "three simple rules" for living longer. T F

4. The way you live can add years to your life (or take years away). T F

5. People in certain countries often live longer than the average. T F

6. How long your family members live has no relationship to how long you will. T F

EXPLORING VOCABULARY

Thinking about the Vocabulary

Which target words and phrases are new to you? Circle them here and in the reading. Then read "Living to 100 and Beyond" again. Look at the context of each new word and phrase. Can you guess the meaning?

Target Words and Phrases			
forever (1)	**possibly** (3)	**treat** (3)	**risks** (4)
likely (2)	**limit** (3)	**as well** (3)	**make a living** (4)
similar (2)	**beyond** (3)	**process** (3)	**injuries** (4)
generally (3)	**made it** (3)	**lifestyle** (4)	**double** (5)

Using the Vocabulary

 These sentences are **about the reading**. Complete them with the target words and phrases in the box.

double	forever	lifestyle	likely	limit	made it
make a living	possibly	process	similar	treat	

1. Some people dream of a life without end. They want to live

   _____.

2. Juan Ponce de Léon probably heard the stories from Asia about a spring with special powers. It is _____ that he heard about it.

3. He also learned about an island with a _____ spring. The two springs were alike.

4. Scientists used to think no one could _____ live more than 120 years. They thought it could not happen in any way.

5. Now, no one thinks of 120 years as the longest anyone can live. No one sees 120 as the _____ anymore.

6. A French woman managed to reach the age of 122. She _____ to 122.

7. Today, doctors can deal with heart problems better. They can give heart patients new kinds of medical help. They can _____ these problems better now.

8. Our bodies change as we grow older. We go through the aging _____, a series of changes, actions, or events.

9. Your _____, or the way you live every day, affects how long you will live.

10. How will you earn enough money to live on? You may live longer if you choose a safe way to _____.

11. Researchers have managed to _____ the lifetimes of certain flies and worms. In other words, they got them to live twice as long as usual.

B These sentences use the target words and phrases **in new contexts.** Complete them with the words and phrases in the box.

double	forever	lifestyle	likely	limit	made her living
make it	possibly	process	similar	treat	

1. The speed _____ on this street is 35 miles per hour.

2. She _____ as a secretary.

3. The train won't leave for an hour. Don't worry, we'll _____ in time.

4. The two companies offer _____ services, so it's hard to choose.

5. I didn't need a doctor. I was able to _____ the cut myself.

6. They promised to _____ his pay, so he agreed to stay.

7. Getting a college degree is a long _____.

8. It's _____ to rain later, so take an umbrella.

9. Having a baby usually causes changes in a couple's _____.

10. The movie had a happy ending. The two main characters promised to love each other _____.

11. If the rent doubles, then I can't _____ afford it!

C Read each definition and look at the paragraph number in parentheses ( ). Look back at the reading to **find the target word or phrase** for each definition. Write it in the chart.

Definition	Target Word or Phrase
1. usually, in most cases (3)	
2. past or later than (a certain time or date) (3)	
3. too, also (3)	
4. chances that something bad may happen (4)	
5. hurt done to the body, as in an accident or an attack (4)	

Building on the Vocabulary

Studying Word Grammar

The adverb *possibly* usually means "perhaps, maybe": *He's going to buy a car soon, possibly this week.*

When *possibly* follows *can't* or *couldn't,* it means "in any way": *I can't possibly get there on time.*

What is the meaning of *possibly* in these sentences? Check (✓) your answers in the chart.

1. I'm sorry, but I couldn't possibly go out tonight.
2. This is possibly your best work ever.
3. You can't possibly mean what you're saying!
4. Is it going to rain? Possibly.

In any way	Perhaps

DEVELOPING YOUR SKILLS

Understanding and Using Supporting Details

A Supply a detail from the reading to support each of the general statements below. Use your own words and write complete sentences.

1. People have told many stories about ways to avoid growing old. For example, _____

    _____

2. Some people have already lived to be more than 120 years old. _____

    _____

    _____

3. There are several reasons why people in many countries live longer lives now. _____

    _____

4. Some things beyond our control affect our life expectancy. _____

    _____

    _____

B Write a general statement that relates to each supporting example.

1. <u>Take care of yourself. / Live a healthy lifestyle.</u> _____

    For example, eat well, get enough sleep and exercise, and don't smoke.

2. _____

    For example, take the bus instead of riding a motorcycle.

3. _____

    Don't choose a dangerous kind of career, like working on a fishing boat at sea.

4. _____

    For example, your hair and eye color depend on them, and about 70% of your life expectancy.

5. _____

    For example, people in Australia and Japan are more likely to make it to 100.

Thinking about the Main Idea

Complete this sentence to give the main idea of "Living to 100 and Beyond."

If you want to _____, then you should
                         (1)

_____ and_____, but a lot depends on
        (2)   **(3)**

your _____, and these you cannot control.
         (4)

Sharing Opinions

Talk about these questions in a small group.

1. Look again at Rules 1, 2, and 3 in the reading. Think about the things these rules say to do. What do you think is simple to do? What is hard?

2. The three rules in the reading say nothing about a person's relationships. Do relationships matter in living a long life? Explain your opinion.

3. The three rules say nothing about a person's state of mind—how he or she thinks and feels. Does this matter in living a long life? Explain your opinion.

4. What do you think the secret is to living a long life?

Using New Words

Work with a partner. Choose five target words or phrases from the list on page 160. On a piece of paper, use each word or phrase in a sentence.

Writing

Choose a topic. Write a paragraph.

1. Would you like to make it to 100 or beyond? Explain why or why not.

2. Imagine that today you celebrated your 100th birthday. Now you are writing in your journal about how you spent your day.

CHAPTER 18

The Placebo Effect

What are they thinking?

GETTING READY TO READ

Talk with a partner or in a small group.

1. When you are sick, what do you usually do? Do you take medicine? Do you see a doctor?

2. When you go to the doctor because you feel sick, do you expect to get a prescription?[1] Explain why or why not.

3. Does a sick person's state of mind (his or her thoughts and emotions) affect how quickly he or she gets well? Explain your answer.

[1] a *prescription* = a doctor's written order for a specific medicine for a sick person

READING

Look at the words and picture next to the reading. Then read without stopping.

The Placebo Effect

1   Harry S. wanted to quit smoking. So, when he saw an **ad** for a study on ways to **break the habit**, he called and offered to be part of it. The study was at a local university, where Harry and the other **volunteers**—all of them people who wanted to stop smoking—were divided into three groups. The volunteers in Group A received nicotine gum.[1] (Nicotine is in tobacco.[2] It is what gives smokers the good feeling they get from smoking.) When these smokers felt the need for a cigarette, they could **chew** a piece of this gum instead. It would give them the nicotine they were used to. The volunteers in Group B, including Harry, got some gum, too. It was just **plain** chewing gum, but the volunteers did not know that. The people in Group C got nothing. A group like this in a study is called the control group.

2   After a four-hour period without cigarettes, Harry and the other volunteers had to write answers to a set of questions. Their answers showed how much they wanted a cigarette at that point. Not surprisingly, the smokers in Group C—the group that got no gum—showed the strongest cravings.[3] The smokers in the other two groups did not feel such a strong need to smoke.

3   What surprised the researchers was that the results for Groups A and B were exactly the same. That meant that the plain chewing gum worked as well as the gum with nicotine. Why? The researchers say, "Maybe it was the placebo effect." In other words, the smokers in Group B *BELIEVED* that the gum would help them feel better, so they did feel better.

4   A placebo is something that seems like a medical **treatment** but does not contain any real medicine. The word *placebo* means "I will please" in Latin. The purpose of a placebo is to please a patient who doesn't really need medicine but wants some. Doctors have given placebos to patients in **situations** like these for hundreds of years. If the patient then feels better, the doctor may say it is because of the placebo effect.

continued

[1] a pack of *gum*

[2] *tobacco* = the plant whose leaves are used to make cigarettes and cigars

[3] a *craving* = a very strong wish for something (such as a certain food)

5   Not everyone believes that the placebo effect **exists**, but researchers in Houston, Texas, have found some interesting evidence[4] for it. They did a study on a certain type of knee **operation**. A lot of people have this operation—about 350,000 a year—and it is expensive, costing about $5,000. The study showed that a **fake** operation worked just as well as the real thing! There were 180 volunteers in the study, and they understood that they might get a real operation or they might not. The ones who had fake surgery[5] got only three small cuts around their knee. After two weeks, most patients believed that their surgery was real. Later, 35–40% of all patients reported that their knees felt better. The numbers were the same for those who had a real operation and those who had the "placebo surgery."

[4] *evidence* = facts that show something is true

6   Some researchers think that the placebo effect works only in a very few situations, possibly only in the case of pain. They have an idea how the placebo effect works in cases like these. According to some **recent** studies, when patients believe they are receiving treatment, their brains produce **natural** painkillers. The brain produces these when a person expects pain to go away. The brain's own painkillers then help **block** the pain.

[5] *surgery* = when a doctor cuts open the body to fix or take out something; an operation

7   Both the smokers in Harry's group and the fake surgery patients felt less pain than expected. Something happened that helped them feel better. Maybe the idea that they were getting treatment (a supply of nicotine or an operation) produced painkillers in their brains. Or perhaps something else was happening. For example, maybe the sugar in the chewing gum helped Harry and the others in his group feel better. Scientists agree that **further** research is needed. **So far**, no one has really **proven** that the placebo effect exists.

Quick Comprehension Check

Read these sentences. Circle T (true) or F (false).

1. Harry's doctor made him be part of a study on quitting smoking.   **T**   **F**

2. Chewing gum helped the smokers go without smoking.   **T**   **F**

3. A placebo has strong drugs in it.   **T**   **F**

4. The placebo effect depends on what a person believes.   **T**   **F**

5. Doctors have done only one study on the placebo effect.   **T**   **F**

6. Some studies show the brain can produce its own painkillers.   **T**   **F**

EXPLORING VOCABULARY

Thinking about the Vocabulary

Which target words and phrases are new to you? Circle them here and in the reading. Then read "The Placebo Effect" again. Look at the context of each new word and phrase. Can you guess the meaning?

Target Words and Phrases			
ad (1)	plain (1)	operation (5)	block (6)
break the habit (1)	treatment (4)	fake (5)	further (7)
volunteers (1)	situations (4)	recent (6)	so far (7)
chew (1)	exists (5)	natural (6)	proven (7)

Using the Vocabulary

 Complete these sentences. Write *an ad, blocking, chewing,* and *an operation.*

1. She's _____.

2. He's _____
   the way in.

3. This is _____
   (short for *advertisement*).

4. They're performing
   _____.

B These sentences are **about the reading**. Complete them with the words and phrases in the box.

break the habit	exist	fake	further	natural	plain
proven	recent	situations	so far	treatment	volunteers

1. For Harry, smoking was a thing he did repeatedly. He wanted to stop this behavior. He wanted to _____ of smoking.

2. The study on smoking used _____, people who offer to do something without expecting pay or anything else.

3. Some volunteers got a special gum with nicotine in it. The other gum was just _____ chewing gum, gum without anything added.

4. Doctors give placebos to patients in certain _____, meaning when certain conditions are present or certain things are happening.

5. Some people believe that the placebo effect doesn't _____. They say there isn't really any effect like this.

6. Some patients got a _____ knee operation. It wasn't a real operation.

7. _____ studies on the brain are studies that happened not long ago.

8. Patients go to doctors to get care or _____ for sickness or injuries.

9. Some painkillers are made by drug companies. The brain produces _____ painkillers.

10. We need more information about the placebo effect, so researchers need to do _____ studies.

11. _____, or until now, no one has really understood the placebo effect.

12. No one has shown clearly that the placebo effect exists. No one has _____ it.

C These sentences use the target words and phrases **in new contexts**. Complete them with the words and phrases in the box.

break the habit	exist	fake	further	natural	plain
proved	recent	situation	so far	treatments	volunteers

1. Red isn't her _____ hair color. She was born with brown hair.

2. These firefighters are _____. They don't get paid.

3. I wish she would _____ of calling me every time she has a problem.

4. She is still in pain from a _____ operation.

5. We haven't had any trouble. Everything has gone smoothly _____.

6. He prefers _____ pizza: just cheese and tomato sauce, nothing else.

7. I _____ to my parents that I could deal with both school and work.

8. We'll make a decision after _____ discussion tomorrow.

9. Doctors are working on new _____ for patients with burns.

10. What is the political _____ in the country at the moment?

11. Dinosaurs[1] no longer _____.

12. When the police caught him, he had several _____ IDs.[2]

[1]*Dinosaurs* lived millions of years ago.   [2]An *ID* is an identification card.

Building on the Vocabulary

Studying Word Grammar

Farther and *further* are both comparative forms of *far*.

- Use *farther* when you mean a longer distance: *They ran/traveled/sailed farther than we did.*

- Use *further* when you refer to time, amounts, or processes: *We need to discuss/look into/study this further.*

These words can be adjectives (*a farther star, further research*) or adverbs (*it spread farther, we'll develop it further*).

A **Complete the sentences with *farther* or *further*.**

1. My classroom is _____ down the hall.

2. I need _____ practice.

3. They never developed the plan any _____.

4. Clear Lake is nicer than Heart Lake, but it's _____ away.

5. You can swim _____ than I can.

6. He will study math _____ when he goes to college.

B **Write your own sentences using *farther* and *further*.**

1. _____

2. _____

DEVELOPING YOUR SKILLS

Paraphrasing and Quoting

The following sentences paraphrase sentences in the reading. (They use different words to say the same thing.) Find the sentence in the reading with the same meaning and copy it here. Use quotation marks (" ") because you are quoting someone else's exact words.

1. The researchers were surprised that Groups A and B showed the same results. "What surprised the researchers was that the results for Groups A and B were exactly the same."

2. Harry S. didn't want to smoke anymore. _____

_____

3. The volunteers in all three groups spent four hours without smoking and then had to answer some questions. _____

_____

4. Scientists think that they need to look into the placebo effect some more.

_____

5. Up to now, no one has shown that there really is such a thing as the placebo effect. _____

_____

Pronoun Reference

Remember: A pronoun takes the place of a noun or a noun phrase. (A noun phrase is a group of words for a person, place, thing, or idea.) A pronoun generally refers back to a noun or noun phrase that came before it.

What do the boldfaced pronouns mean in these sentences? Look back at the reading.

1. Paragraph 1: . . . he called and offered to be part of **it**. _____
2. Paragraph 1: **It** is what gives smokers the good feeling they get . . .

_____

3. Paragraph 3: . . . , so **they** did feel better. _____
4. Paragraph 5: . . . researchers in Houston, Texas, have found some interesting evidence for **it**. _____
5. Paragraph 5: The numbers were the same for **those** who had a real operation . . . _____
6. Paragraph 6: The brain produces **these** when a person expects pain to go away. _____

Discussion

Talk about these questions in a small group.

1. What was the purpose of the first study described in the reading? How were the three groups different? What surprised the researchers and why?

2. What was the purpose of the second study? How were the two groups different? What were the results?

3. Imagine that you are invited to be part of a study on a new drug. The drug is supposed to strengthen a person's memory and make him or her smarter. Some of the volunteers will get the drug, and some will get a placebo. Would you volunteer? Explain your answer.

Using New Words

Ask and answer these questions with a partner. Use one of the words or phrases in parentheses. Then talk about your answers with the class.

1. When have you (tried to/managed to) **break a bad habit**?

2. What **ad** on TV do you really (like/hate)?

3. (When/Where) are **volunteers** usually needed?

4. What are two things besides foods that (people/animals) sometimes **chew**?

5. What famous (person/thing) doesn't really **exist**?

Writing

Choose a topic. Write a paragraph.

1. Answer question 3 from **Discussion** above.

2. When do you go see a doctor? How do you feel about going to doctors?

CHAPTER 19

Tears

Why the tears?

GETTING READY TO READ

Talk with a partner or in a small group.

1. When was the last time you cried? Why did you cry?
2. When is it OK to cry? Are there times when a person *should* cry?
3. Do you agree with a, b, or c? Choose one and explain your choice.
   a. Crying is a healthy thing to do.
   b. Crying is bad for you.
   c. Crying doesn't help you or hurt you either.

READING

Look at the words and pictures next to the reading. Then read without stopping.

Tears

1   Tears are good for your eyes. In fact, without them, your eyes wouldn't even be able to move. Some people say tears help us in other ways, too. Maybe you know someone who likes to watch sad movies in order to "have a good cry." It hasn't been proven, but tears may be good not only for your eyes but for your emotional health as well.

2   We generally only notice tears when we cry, but we have them in our eyes all the time. Tears affect how we see the world while at the same time protecting our eyes from it. Without this **liquid** covering them, our eyes would be at risk of infection.[1] In addition, we need tears in order to see. The cornea[2] of the eye does not have a perfectly smooth **surface**. Tears **fill in** the **holes** in the cornea and make it smooth so that we can see clearly. Without tears, the world would look very strange to us.

3   There are three types of tears, and they are called basal, reflex, and emotional (or psychic) tears. These three types are different not only in purpose but also in composition.[3]

- Basal tears are the ones that we produce all the time. On average, our eyes produce these tears at a rate of five to ten ounces[4] a day. When we blink our eyes (quickly close and open them), we spread basal tears across the surface of our eyes. If we don't blink enough, like some people who spend long hours in front of a computer, then our eyes get dry.

- Have you ever cut up an onion[5] and felt tears come to your eyes? Tears of that type are called reflex tears. They are the ones that fill our eyes when a cold wind **blows**. These tears also protect our eyes, washing away **dust** and other **materials** that get into them.

- Emotional, or psychic, tears **flow** when we feel certain emotions. When we cry tears of sadness, disappointment, or happiness, we are crying emotional tears. Emotional tears are the tears we think of when we use the word *cry*.

continued

[1] *infection* = sickness in a part of the body

[2] the *cornea* = a covering for the eye; see the picture on the following page

[3] *composition* = the way something is made up of different things, parts, etc.

[4] an *ounce* = a small amount of liquid (eight ounces = one measuring cup)

[5] an *onion*

4   Tom Lutz, the author of *Crying: The Natural and Cultural History of Tears,* writes, "**Throughout** history, and in every culture, . . . everyone, everywhere cries at some time." Even men and women who say they never cry can usually remember crying as children. Most of us probably think it is **normal** for men or women to cry at certain times, and at such times, we may even **encourage** them to cry. For example, it is no surprise when someone cries during a sad movie, and we often expect people to cry when a family member dies. However, we don't always take this **view** of tears. Sometimes adults who cry—or even children who do—lose the respect of others. For example, what would you think of an adult who cried over losing a card game? Most people are **aware** of the social rules about when, where, and why it is OK to cry. These rules generally **differ** for children and adults, and often for men and women. They depend on things such as family, culture, and religion, and they change over time.

5   Some people think it is not just OK to cry but actually healthy to let the tears flow. Doctors in Greece over 2,500 years ago thought that tears came from the brain and that everyone needed to let them out. Today, many people still believe in[6] getting tears out. They say that through crying, we get rid of emotions we have stored up, which is good for our **mental** health. Some people report that they feel better after crying. This could be because of the **chemicals** in emotional tears. One chemical is a type of endorphin, a painkiller that the body naturally produces. Emotional tears increase the amount of endorphin that gets to the brain because tears flow from the eye into the nose and pass to the brain that way. This painkiller may make a person less aware of sad or angry feelings, and that could explain why someone feels better after "a good cry."

[6] *believe in* = trust in, feel sure that (a person or thing) is good

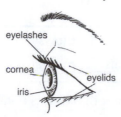

Front view of an eye   Side view of an eye

eyebrow
eyelid
tear
tear duct

eyelashes
cornea
iris
eyelids

Tom Lutz's words come from *Crying: The Natural and Cultural History of Tears* (New York: W.W. Norton & Company, 1999), 17.

Quick Comprehension Check

Read these sentences. Circle T (true) or F (false).

1. Tears are important for keeping our eyes healthy.   T   F

2. Tears are important for our ability to see.   T   F

3. There are two different kinds of tears.   T   F

4. We have emotional tears in our eyes all the time.   T   F

5. People generally have the same ideas about when it is   T   F
   OK to cry.

6. Some people think it can be good for you to cry.   T   F

EXPLORING VOCABULARY

Thinking about the Vocabulary

Which target words and phrases are new to you? Circle them here and in the reading. Then read "Tears" again. Look at the context of each new word and phrase. Can you guess the meaning?

Target Words and Phrases			
liquid (2)	blows (3)	throughout (4)	aware (4)
surface (2)	dust (3)	normal (4)	differ (4)
fill in (2)	materials (3)	encourage (4)	mental (5)
holes (2)	flow (3)	view (4)	chemicals (5)

Using the Vocabulary

 A These sentences are **about the reading**. Complete them with the words and phrases in the box.

are encouraging	aware of	blows	chemicals	dust
flow	materials	mental	normal	surface

1. The eye looks perfectly smooth, but it is not. Its _____ is irregular, with tiny holes and wrinkles (like your skin when you look at it closely).

2. When a wind _____ cold air into your eyes, they fill with reflex tears.

3. Sometimes you might get _____ in your eyes. It could happen when you are driving on a dry dirt road or cleaning under your bed.

4. Tears help wash away dust, dirt, sand, or any other _____ that might get into your eyes.

5. When you feel certain emotions, tears may start to _____, like water moving in a river.

6. At certain times it is not strange for someone to cry. It is _____. Everyone expects it.

7. People may tell someone, "Go ahead and cry." They _____ the person to cry.

8. Most people are _____ the social rules for crying. They know about them.

9. Tears are good for your eyes and may be good for your _____ health, too, meaning your emotions and state of mind.

10. There are different substances in the three types of tears. The _____ in emotional tears include a painkiller.

B These sentences use the target words **in new contexts**. Complete them with the words in the box.

aware	blew	chemicals	dust	encouraged
flows	materials	mental	normal	surface

1. The river _____ to the sea.
2. Only a few people have walked on the _____ of the moon.
3. The teacher's fingers were white with _____ from writing on the blackboard with a piece of chalk.
4. A strong wind _____ his hat off.
5. Ann says, "I have a _____ block against math. I don't understand it or enjoy it, and I never will."
6. It's _____ to feel nervous during a job interview.
7. To build a good house, you have to start with good-quality building _____.
8. There's a lot he doesn't notice. I bet he isn't _____ of her feelings for him.
9. My parents _____ me to think it over before deciding.
10. There are strong _____ in some of the cleaning products in the kitchen.

C **Read these sentences. Write the boldfaced target words or phrases next to their definitions.**

a. We need to dig a deep **hole** to plant the tree.
b. Water can take the form of a **liquid**, a gas, or a solid (ice).
c. I cried **throughout** the movie, from beginning to end.
d. The two companies **differ** in how they treat their employees.
e. Who did he vote for? Do you know his political **views**?
f. There is a bad hole in the street. Somebody should **fill it in**.

Target Words/Phrases   **Definitions**

1. _____ = be different or not alike

2. _____ = a substance that can flow and be poured

3. _____ = during all of a period of time

4. _____ = an open or empty space in something solid

5. _____ = opinions or beliefs

6. _____ = put something in a hole in order to make a smooth surface

Building on the Vocabulary

Studying Collocations

The noun *view* has different meanings:

- *View* often means "opinion, belief." Use *take* or *hold* with *view* to mean "have an opinion": *He takes the view that children should be seen and not heard.*

- *View* can also mean "the area someone can see." Use *have* with *view* when it has this meaning: *He has a view of the park from his house.*

A **Complete the following sentences. Make true statements.**

1. _____ and I hold similar views on _____.
    (name)
2. From my _____ window, I have a view of _____.
        (room)

B **Write two more sentences with *view*.**

1. _____

2. _____

DEVELOPING YOUR SKILLS

Paraphrasing and Quoting

A Answer each question by copying a sentence from "Tears." Use quotation marks (" ") before and after the sentence.

1. What would happen if we did not have tears in our eyes?

   "Without this liquid covering them, our eyes would be at risk of infection."

2. How do tears help us see clearly?

   _____

   _____

   _____

3. What are the different types of tears?

   _____

   _____

   _____

4. Social rules about crying differ for children vs. adults and often for men vs. women. What else affects the rules?

   _____

   _____

   _____

5. What effect does the painkiller endorphin possibly have on a person?

   _____

   _____

   _____

B On a piece of paper, write answers to these questions. Do not copy sentences from the reading. You will need to paraphrase (use your own words).

1. How do tears help our eyes?

2. When do our eyes produce basal, reflex, and emotional tears?

3. How does a person learn the social rules about crying?

4. Why do some people believe it is good to cry?

Summarizing

On a piece of paper, write a one-paragraph summary of "Tears." Include the answers to these questions:

- What are tears good for?
- Which kinds of tears protect our eyes?
- Which kind of tears do you produce when we cry?
- What do social rules about crying tell us?
- What do some people believe about crying?

Sharing Opinions

1. Check (✓) your answers to the questions below. Add a situation of your own to the list. Then share answers with a partner. Ask your partner about the situation you added.

Is it OK for a person to cry:

	An adult		A child	
	Yes	No	Yes	No

   a. at the movies?

   b. when his/her team loses a game?

   c. when something bad happens at work/at school?

   d. when saying good-bye at the airport?

   e. at a religious service for someone who has died?

   f. _____?

2. Do you think there are differences between the social rules about crying for men and those for women? Fill in the chart with situations. Compare charts with your partner.

When is it OK to cry?

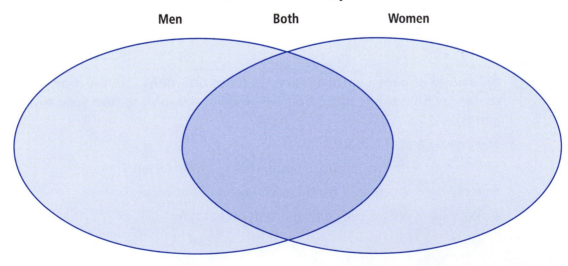

Men   Both   Women

Using New Words

Work with a partner. Choose five target words or phrases from the list on page 176. On a piece of paper, use each word or phrase in a sentence.

Writing

Choose a topic. Write a paragraph.

1. Do you remember crying as a child? Describe an experience that made you cry.

2. Is there someone in your life who encourages you to do things? For example:

   My friends encourage me to believe in myself.

   My father always encouraged me to get a good education.

   Describe the encouragement you have received from someone and its influence on you.

CHAPTER 20

Bionic Men and Women

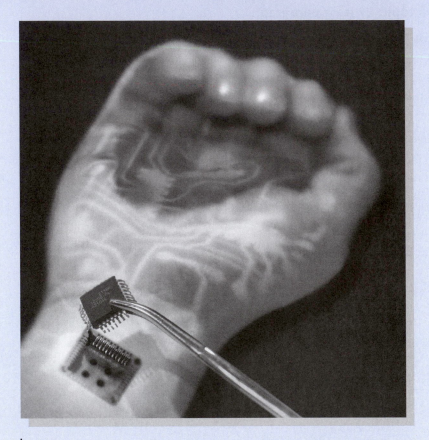

A hand of the future?

GETTING READY TO READ

Talk in a small group or with your class.

1. What movies or TV shows have you seen about a person who was part machine? What was the story about?

2. When a part of someone's body stops working, the person's life may depend on a machine, whether in the hospital or in everyday life. Give an example of a situation like this.

READING

Look at the words and pictures next to the reading. Then read without stopping.

Bionic Men and Women

1   In the movie *Star Wars: The Empire Strikes Back,* Luke Skywalker loses a hand, but he gets a new one, an **artificial** hand that looks and works just like a real one. This is not unusual in movies that take place far into the future. It is easy to believe that 100 years from now, doctors will be able to **replace** body parts with machines. But you don't have to go to the movies to see this happen.

2   Machines are already doing the jobs of various human body parts. There are people who can see, hear, walk, or pick up their children because of artificial eyes, ears, legs, and arms. These are all possible because of **developments** in the field of science called bionics. *Bionics* means the study of how living things are made and how they work. **Engineers** study bionics in order to **design** machines that are similar to living things. For example, in order to design airplanes, they have studied birds. The field of bionics also includes building machines to replace parts of the body or to support processes **within** the body.

3   One example of a bionic device[1] is the pacemaker. Doctors can put a pacemaker into the **chest** of someone whose heart **beats** too slowly or not regularly enough. They **attach** the pacemaker to the heart with wires, and the device gets its power from a **battery**. The wires carry small amounts of electricity to the heart and keep it beating as it should. Many thousands of people depend on pacemakers.

4   Other bionic devices, like Luke Skywalker's new hand, take the place of a body part. A **major** problem in developing bionic parts has been setting up communication between the body and the machine. Normally, the brain tells parts of the body what to do by sending messages along nerves.[2] For example, your brain might send a message to your hand telling it to pick up a pen and write something. But how would it tell an artificial hand to do that? Dr. William

continued

[1] a *device* = a small machine or tool that does a special job

[2] *nerves* = thin parts like lines throughout the body that carry information to/from the brain

Craelius, who has invented an artificial hand, says, "Communication is **key**, and it is getting easier."

5   Machines are not the only things that can replace a body part. There are also transplants. A transplant is an operation to move a body part, such as a heart or a kidney,[3] from one person to another. One major problem with transplants is that there aren't enough hearts, kidneys, and so on, available, so hospitals cannot **keep up with** the **demand** for transplants. Patients have to wait, and some have no time left. **Therefore**, many scientists see bionics as the best hope for the future. Using bionics, a patient could get a new heart or kidney right away instead of waiting for a transplant. Other scientists disagree. They say that bionics is already a thing of the past, and they have a better idea: They are working on ways to use animal parts for transplants.

6   Maybe in the future our choices won't be limited to bionic body parts and transplant operations. Maybe science will take us in another direction. Consider these facts: When a salamander[4] loses a leg, it can grow a new one, and if an earthworm[5] is cut in two pieces, the piece with the head can grow a new tail. Wouldn't it be great if a person who lost a hand or a kidney could grow a new one? This may sound like something from another sci-fi[6] movie, but it could happen. Researchers are now studying the genes[7] that let salamanders grow new legs, and they hope to learn how humans might do the same thing.

7   Growing a new body part could be the best way to go. On the other hand, some people might prefer bionic body parts if they had the choice. In the sci-fi movie *RoboCop,* a police officer has an operation that **turns him into** a cyborg—half man, half machine. His new body parts give him special powers, including superhuman strength. Think about it. If bionics could turn you into a superman, what would you do?

Dr. Craelius's words come from the article "Inventor of Artificial Hand Sees 'Bionic' Replacement Parts Becoming More Human," *Medical Devices & Surgical Technology Week* (March 10, 2002), 3.

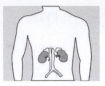

[3] the *kidneys*

[4] a *salamander*

[5] an *earthworm*

[6] *sci-fi* = (informal) *science fiction,* stories about imaginary worlds or imaginary developments in science

[7] *genes* = the parts of cells in your body that control qualities you get from your parents

Quick Comprehension Check

Read these sentences. Circle T (true) or F (false).

1. People can get new body parts only in the movies.   T   F

2. Bionics means studying living things: how they are made   T   F
   and how they work.

3. Giving a man a pacemaker for his heart is an example of   T   F
   using bionics.

4. Machines are our only hope for new body parts in the future.   T   F

5. Some animals can grow new body parts if they need to.   T   F

6. In the movies, bionic body parts sometimes give people   T   F
   special abilities.

EXPLORING VOCABULARY

Thinking about the Vocabulary

Which target words and phrases are new to you? Circle them here and in the reading. Then read "Bionic Men and Women" again. Look at the context of each new word and phrase. Can you guess the meaning?

Target Words and Phrases

artificial (1)	design (2)	attach (3)	keep up with (5)
replace (1)	within (2)	battery (3)	demand (5)
developments (2)	chest (3)	major (4)	therefore (5)
engineers (2)	beats (3)	key (4)	turns him into (7)

Using the Vocabulary

A These sentences are about the reading. What is the meaning of each **boldfaced** word or phrase? Circle a, b, or c.

1. Some people have to get **artificial** eyes, ears, hands, and legs. *Artificial* means:

   a. not available   **b.** not natural   **c.** not connected

2. People sometimes **design** machines to work like living things. *Design* means:

   a. draw plans for   **b.** deal in   **c.** take over

3. A machine may be needed to support a process **within** the body. *Within* means:

   a. beyond   **b.** according to   **c.** inside

4. A healthy heart **beats** slowly when a person is resting. *Beats* means:

   a. makes a regular movement   **b.** makes a living   **c.** makes an investment

5. Doctors **attach** a pacemaker to a heart with wires. *Attach* means:

   a. block   **b.** connect   **c.** avoid

6. A pacemaker gets its power from a **battery**. A *battery* is:

   a. a kind of software   **b.** a thing that provides electricity   **c.** a volunteer

7. The body and the bionic body part must communicate. Communication is **key**. *Key* means:

   a. necessary for success   **b.** not likely to exist   **c.** worth nothing

8. There is a great **demand** for transplants. *Demand* means:

   a. the lifestyle people want   **b.** the materials people use   **c.** the need people have

9. Transplants aren't always possible when patients need them. **Therefore**, some people think bionics offers more hope for the future. *Therefore* means:

   a. right away   **b.** because   **c.** for that reason

10. In the movie *RoboCop*, an operation **turned** a man **into** a cyborg. *Turn* (a person or thing) *into* (someone or something else) means:

    a. change into   **b.** chew up   **c.** fill in

B These sentences use the target words and phrases **in new contexts**. Complete them with the words and phrases in the box.

artificial	attach	battery	beat	demand
designed	key	therefore	turns them into	within

1. She _____ and made her own clothes.
2. Please _____ a recent photo to your application.
3. The restaurant had _____ flowers on the tables.
4. Our hotel was _____ walking distance of the city center.
5. My little radio isn't working. It needs a new _____.
6. His heart _____ faster when he saw her.
7. The _____ thing is for the patient to believe in the treatment.
8. The army claims that it takes boys and _____ men.
9. The plan presented too many risks. _____, he decided against it.
10. The company went out of business because there wasn't enough _____ for their products.

C Read these sentences. Write the **boldfaced** target words or phrases next to their definitions.

a. They want to **replace** their old car.
b. Recent **developments** in medical research encourage us to hope.
c. The computer, automobile, and airline industries all employ **engineers**.
d. The young father held his baby against his **chest**.
e. We couldn't **keep up with** the other runners, so we gave up.
f. The country has just two **major** political parties.

Target Words/Phrases   Definitions

1. _____ = change (one person or thing for another)
2. _____ = large or important
3. _____ = changes that make something more advanced
4. _____ = people who design machines, roads, bridges, etc.
5. _____ = move as fast or do as much (as someone else)
6. _____ = the front part of a person's body between the neck and the stomach

Building on the Vocabulary

> ### Studying Collocations
>
> Remember: Certain prepositions often follow certain adjectives. Use:
>
> *aware* + *of*
> *key* + *to*
> *normal* + *for*
> *similar* + *to*

A **Complete each sentence with a preposition.**

1. Certain players have been key _____ the success of the team.

2. He is aware _____ the risks of smoking.

3. The child's eating habits are normal _____ his age.

4. Her situation is similar _____ yours.

B **Write a sentence using each adjective + preposition in Part A.**

1. _____

2. _____

3. _____

4. _____

DEVELOPING YOUR SKILLS

Paraphrasing and Quoting

A **Answer the questions by copying sentences from "Bionic Men and Women." Use quotation marks (" ") before and after the sentences.**

1. What has happened thanks to developments in the field of bionics?

   "There are people who _____

   _____."

2. Why has it been so hard to develop things like artificial hands?

   _____

   _____

3. What is a transplant?

   _____

   _____

4. Why are researchers studying salamanders?

_____

_____

B **Answer these questions without copying sentences from the reading. You will need to paraphrase.**

1. What is a pacemaker? What does it do? _____

_____

_____

_____

2. What is one problem with transplants? _____

_____

_____

_____

3. Why might some people like the idea of getting bionic body parts? _____

_____

_____

_____

Summarizing

On a piece of paper, write a one-paragraph summary of "Bionic Men and Women." Include the answers to the following questions:
- What does _bionics_ mean? (Copy the definition from the reading and use quotation marks around it.)
- How do bionic devices help people?
- What is another way to replace a body part that isn't working?
- What other way to replace body parts may be possible in the future?

Role-playing

Form a small group. Two of you are scientists. You work in the field of bionics. The rest of you are reporters, and you are here to interview the scientists about the most recent developments in their work. The reporters ask questions. The scientists answer the questions and ask their own questions. For example:

REPORTER: What are you working on right now?

SCIENTIST: We are developing a new . . .

Using New Words

Work with a partner. Take turns asking for and giving information.

1. Name two things that can run on **batteries**.
2. Name two things that **designers** work on.
3. Name two things that **engineers** work on.
4. Name two things that are **key** to doing well in school.
5. Describe something old that you'd like to **replace**.

Writing

Choose a topic. Write a paragraph.

1. Imagine that you could replace some part or parts of your body with artificial part(s) that would give you super powers, special powers that humans don't normally have. What would you replace and why?
2. Would you like a career as a designer or an engineer of some kind? Explain.

Wrap-up

REVIEWING VOCABULARY

A Where would you find . . .

  __d__   **1.** a battery?   **a.** under a bed

_____ **2.** an ad?   **b.** in a science lab

_____ **3.** dust?   **c.** in the newspaper

_____ **4.** chemicals?   **d.** in a clock

B Complete the phrase.

1. Write the noun *living, operation, risk,* or *treatment.*

    a. perform an ____ *operation* ____

    b. make a _____

    c. take a _____

    d. provide _____

2. Write the verb *blow, chew, replace,* or *treat.*

    a. _____ an injury

    b. _____ your food

    c. _____ your nose

    d. _____ a broken TV

3. Write the noun *chest, habit,* or *hole.*

    a. a deep _____

    b. a bad _____

    c. a hairy _____

4. Write the adjective *artificial, further, mental,* or *smooth.*

    a. _____ health

    b. _____ flowers

    c. _____ developments

    d. _____ surfaces

EXPANDING VOCABULARY

A We can add the prefix *un-* to *aware*, *likely*, and *natural* to form adjectives with the opposite meaning. Other prefixes can also mean "not."

Combine the prefixes meaning "not" with the adjectives in the box. Complete the sentences with the new words.

| **un-** + aware   **un-** + likely   **un-** + natural   **ab-** + normal   **dis-** + similar |

1. Her hair was an _____unnatural_____ red.

2. The sky is perfectly clear, so I think it is _____ to rain.

3. The two scientists used the same process but had _____
   results.

4. He is _____ of the problem. Someone has to tell him.

5. My cat's _____ behavior made me think she was sick.

B Sometimes a noun and a verb in the same word family look alike: *They* **design** *buildings. They showed us a* **design** *for a new house.* Sometimes they don't look alike: *He* **injured** *his leg. It was a serious* **injury**.

Read the following sentences and find the noun and verb from the same family. Complete the chart.

Nouns	Verbs
attachment	attach

1. **a.** Attach one wire to each end of the battery.
   b. There is a strong attachment between the two sisters.
2. **a.** The players differ in their natural abilities.
   b. There are many differences between the two schools.
3. **a.** I encouraged him to see a doctor.
   b. Her friends gave her lots of encouragement.

Nouns	Verbs

4. a. What is the speed limit on this road?
   b. The school limits classes to no more than 15 students.
5. a. They hope to slow down the aging process.
   b. The factory processes fresh fruit. They put it in cans.
6. a. He will have to prove that he can do the work.
   b. A photo ID or passport shows proof of who you are.
7. a. Who will replace the director if she leaves?
   b. Our regular secretary is on vacation, but her replacement is doing a fine job.

C **Write seven sentences with the noun or verb from each family in Part B.**

1. _____

2. _____

3. _____

4. _____

5. _____

6. _____

7. _____

PLAYING WITH WORDS

Complete the sentences with words you studied in Chapters 17–20. Write the words in the puzzle.

Across

1. I'll love you *forever*_____.

3. The baby slept **t**_____ the trip.

6. What **m**_____ is the jacket made of?

8. Water is a **l**_____.

9. He couldn't prove it. **T**_____, no one believed him.

12. We can't let the party go on **b**_____ midnight.

13. We all agree the problem **e**_____.

Down

2. She's a **v**_____ at the hospital.

4. What would you do if you were in my **s**_____?

5. We watched the river **f**_____.

6. The **m**_____ problem is not enough money.

7. He lives **w**_____ a mile of his job.

10. I can't tell if it's real or **f**_____.

11. He's a **k**_____ member of the team.

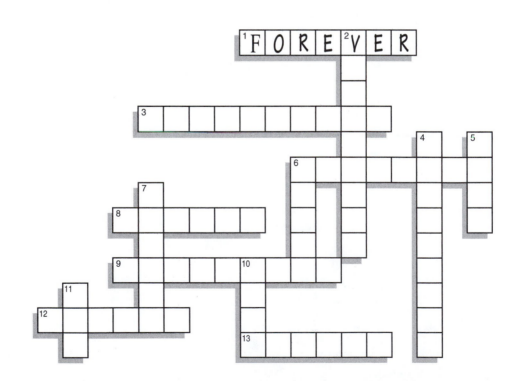

BUILDING DICTIONARY SKILLS

Finding the Correct Meaning

Many words have more than one meaning. Look at the dictionary entries below. Read each sentence and write the number of the meaning.

1. a. __3__ The waves beat against the rocks.

    b. ____ Beat the eggs before you add the flour.

    c. ____ We beat them by a score of 3 to 1.

    d. ____ My heart was beating very quickly.

    e. ____ It's a crime to attack or beat someone.

> **beat**[1] /bit/ *v* **beat, beat, beaten**
> **1** ▸ DEFEAT ◂ [T] to defeat someone in a game, competition etc., or to do better than someone or something: *Stein **beat** me **at** chess in 44 moves.* | *Hank Aaron finally **beat the record** for home runs set by Babe Ruth.*
> **2** ▸ HIT SB ◂ [T] to hit someone many times with your hand, a stick etc.: *He used to come home drunk and beat us.*
> **3** ▸ HIT STH ◂ [I,T] to hit something regularly or continuously: *waves **beating on/against** the shore*
> **4** ▸ FOOD ◂ [I,T] to mix foods together quickly using a fork or a special kitchen tool: *Beat the eggs and add them to the sugar mixture.*
> **5** ▸ SOUND ◂ [I,T] to make a regular sound or movement, or to make something do this: *My heart seemed to be beating much too fast. . . .*

2. a. ____ You have no right to make demands like that.

    b. ____ The baker couldn't keep up with the demand for his bread.

    c. ____ He's in great demand as a speaker.

> **de·mand**[1] /di'mænd/ *n* **1** [singular, U] the need or desire that people have for particular goods or services: *There isn't any **demand for** leaded gas anymore.* **2** a strong request that shows you believe you have the right to get what you ask for: *Union members will strike until the company agrees to their demands.* **3 be in demand** to be wanted by a lot of people: *She's **been in great demand** ever since her book was published.* —see also DEMANDS

3. a. ____ What's the best way to treat a burn?

    b. ____ Don't treat me like a child.

    c. ____ We must treat this situation carefully.

    d. ____ They have to treat the water before people can drink it.

    e. ____ They treated the children to ice cream.

> **treat**[1] /trit/ *v* [T] **1** to behave toward someone in a particular way: *Why do you **treat** me **like** an idiot?* | *She **treats** the children **the same as** adults.* | *Mr. Parker **treats** everyone **equally/fairly**.* **2** to consider something in a particular way: *You can **treat** these costs **as** business expenses.* **3** to give someone medical attention for a sickness or injury: *Eleven people were **treated for** minor injuries.* **4** to buy or arrange something special for someone: *We're **treating** Mom **to** dinner for her birthday.* **5** to put a special substance on something or use a chemical process in order to protect or clean it: *The wood has been treated to make it waterproof.*

UNIT 6

EXPLORING TECHNOLOGY

CHAPTER 21

A History of Telling Time

An atomic clock

GETTING READY TO READ

Talk with the whole class.

1. How many people in the class wear watches? What other ways are there to find out the time?

2. How many times a day do you look to see what time it is? What is the average for the class?

   a. 0–5   **b.** 5–10   **c.** more than 10

3. Do you agree with either of these ideas? Explain.

   a. Life without clocks would be beautiful.

   b. Life without clocks would be terrible.

READING

Look at the words and pictures next to the reading. Then read without stopping. Don't worry about new words. Don't stop to use a dictionary. Just keep reading!

A History of Telling Time

1   No one knows when people first thought about **measuring** time. We do know that they measured it by the sun, moon, and stars, and that they first divided time into months, seasons, and years. Later, they began dividing the day into parts, like hours and minutes, and they developed simple **technology** to help them do this. Today, we have much more advanced ways to tell time, such as the atomic clock pictured on page 197, and we can measure even tiny parts of a second. A great many things have changed in how people tell time—but not everything.

2   The Sumerians, who lived in the area of present-day Iraq, were the first to divide the day into parts. Then five or six thousand years ago, people in North Africa and the Middle East developed ways to tell the time of day. They needed clocks because organized religious and social activities had become part of their cultures. They needed to plan their days and **set** times to meet.

3   Among the first clocks were Egyptian obelisks.[1] The Egyptians used the movement of an obelisk's **shadow** to divide the day into morning and afternoon. Later, they placed stones on the ground around an obelisk to mark **equal** periods of time during the day, the way that numbers do on the face of a clock. That worked **fairly** well, but people could not carry obelisks with them. So the Egyptians invented something **portable**, a kind of sundial[2] that is now called a shadow clock. This came into use about 3,500 years ago, around 1500 B.C.E.[3]

4   There were many types of sundials in Egypt and in other areas around the Mediterranean Sea. All of them, of course, depended on the sun, which was no help in telling time at night. Among the first clocks that did not depend on the sun were water clocks. There were various types of these, too. Some were designed so that water would **drip** at a **constant**

continued

[1] an *obelisk*

[2] one kind of *sundial*

[3] *B.C.E.* = Before the Common Era (also written *B.C.*, "before Christ")

rate from a tiny hole in the bottom of a **container**. Others were designed to have a container slowly fill with water, again at a constant rate. It took a certain amount of time for the container to empty or fill up. However, the flow of water was hard to control, so these clocks were not very **accurate**, and people still did not have a clock they could put in their **pocket**. Hourglasses[4] filled with sand had similar problems.

[4] an *hourglass*

5   In the early 1300s, the first mechanical clocks—machines that measured and told the time—appeared in public buildings in Italy. Nearly 200 years later, around 1500, a German inventor, Peter Henlein, invented a mechanical clock that was powered by a spring.[5] Now clocks were getting smaller and easier to carry, but they still were not very accurate. Then in 1656, the Dutch scientist Christiaan Huygens invented a clock that was a big **step** forward. This was the first pendulum clock.[6] A pendulum moves from side to side, again and again, at a constant rate. Counting the movements of a pendulum was a better way to keep time. Huygens's first pendulum clock kept the time accurately to within one minute a day.

[5] two *springs*

6   Developments in clock technology continued as the demand for clocks increased. People began to need clocks for factories, **transportation**, banking, communications, and so on. Today, much of **modern** life happens at high speed and depends on having the exact time. We also have to have international agreement on what the exact time is.

[6] A grandfather clock is an example of a *pendulum* clock

7   Now we have atomic clocks, and the best of these are accurate to about one-tenth of a nanosecond[7] a day. But even with these **high-tech** clocks, we still measure a year by the time it takes the earth to go around the sun, as people did long, long ago. We say that it takes 365 days, but that is not exactly true. A year is actually a little longer—365.242 days, or 365 days and almost six hours long. So we generally add a day, February 29, every fourth year, and we call those years *leap years*. However, this creates another problem. The extra hours in four years add up to less than 24, so adding one day every fourth year would give us too many days. Therefore, when a year ends in -00 (for example, 1800, 1900, or 2000), we do not always make it a leap year. We do it only when we can divide the year by 4, as in 1600 and 2000. Remember that when you set your watch for the year 2100!

[7] a *nanosecond* = 1/1,000,000,000 (one-billionth) of a second

Quick Comprehension Check

Read these sentences. Circle T (true) or F (false).

1. People first measured time by the sun, moon, and stars.   T   F

2. People invented ways to tell time so they would know
   when to meet.   T   F

3. Water clocks depended on the sun.   T   F

4. Knowing the exact time is more important today than it
   was long ago.   T   F

5. Clocks have not changed in the last 200 years.   T   F

6. The earth takes exactly 365 days to circle the sun.   T   F

EXPLORING VOCABULARY

Thinking about the Vocabulary

Which target words are new to you? Circle them here and in the reading. Then read "A History of Telling Time" again. Look at the context of each new word. Can you guess the meaning?

Target Words			
measuring (1)	equal (3)	constant (4)	step (5)
technology (1)	fairly (3)	container (4)	transportation (6)
set (2)	portable (3)	accurate (4)	modern (6)
shadow (3)	drip (4)	pocket (4)	high-tech (7)

Using the Vocabulary

A **Complete the sentences. Write *containers*, *pockets*, *shadows*, and *transportation*.**

1. You see _____ on
   a sunny day.

2. These are _____.

3. He has _____.

4. These are forms of _____.

These sentences are about the reading. Complete them with the target words in the box.

accurate	constant	dripped	equal	fairly	high-tech
measure	modern	portable	set	step	technology

1. We use clocks to _____ time—to tell how much time has passed or how much time we have.

2. Thousands of years ago, people began developing the _____ for making clocks. (This word refers to the information, tools, and materials used to do something.)

3. As cultures became more advanced, people planned religious or social activities. They needed to _____, or decide on, specific times to meet.

4. The shadow of an obelisk took the same amount of time to move from each stone to the next. The stones marked _____ periods of time.

5. This way of telling time worked _____ well (less than "extremely well" or even "very well").

6. No one could carry an obelisk; obelisks were not _____. People wanted something they could carry.

7. Some water clocks were designed so that water _____, or fell little by little, from a tiny hole.

8. The water in a water clock would drip at a _____ rate. It never speeded up or slowed down.

9. Water clocks and hourglasses did not measure time exactly. They were not very _____.

10. In 1656, there was an important development. The invention of the pendulum clock was a big _____ forward.

11. The phrase _____ *life* refers to the way people live now or have lived in recent times.

12. Some clocks use very advanced technology, so we call them _____ clocks.

These sentences use the target words **in new contexts**. Complete them with the words in the box.

accurate	constant	dripping	equal	fairly	high-tech
measure	modern	portable	set	step	technology

1. I have an old _____ radio that I take to the beach.

2. Getting married is a major _____ in anyone's life.

3. The course is on _____ Chinese history, just the last 100 years.

4. You won't believe all the things his new phone can do. It is very

   _____.

5. When you make a cake, you have to _____ the flour carefully.

6. He is studying computer _____. He wants to be an engineer.

7. They are going to get married some time next spring, but they have not

   _____ the date yet.

8. She does the same work he does, so they should get _____ pay.

9. Her Spanish isn't perfect, but she speaks it _____ well.

10. The shower in the upstairs bathroom won't stop _____. Can
    you fix it?

11. He gave the police an _____ report of the accident.

12. I drove the whole way there at a _____ speed of 55
    miles per hour.

Building on the Vocabulary

Studying Word Grammar

The **root** of the words *portable* and *transportation* is **port**. It comes from a Latin word meaning "carry." Something that is portable is something you can carry. *Transportation* refers to the process or business of carrying people and goods to other places. The verb form is *transport: We transported the computers by truck.*

Choose your own ways to complete the following sentences.

1. The first _____ were not portable, but now people can buy
   portable ones.

2. Modern transportation includes _____, _____, and

   _____.

3. In my country, businesses often transport goods by _____.

DEVELOPING YOUR SKILLS

Scanning

A **Read these statements about "A History of Telling Time." Scan the reading for the information you need to complete them.**

1. People in _____ and _____ were the first to develop ways to tell the time of day.

2. People started needing clocks and setting times to meet after they developed _____ and _____.

3. Obelisks and _____ depended on the sun.

4. A _____ measured time by emptying or filling up with water at a constant rate.

5. The first accurate clock was a _____ clock, invented in _____.

6. The best atomic clocks are accurate to _____.

7. It takes _____ days and _____ hours for the earth to travel around the sun.

8. A year with 366 days is called a _____.

B **Scan the reading for these developments. Number them in chronological order from 1 (the earliest) to 8 (the most recent).**

_____ Countries around the world had to agree on the exact time.

_____ People measured time by the sun, moon, and stars.

_____ Peter Henlein invented a spring-powered clock.

_____ The Egyptian shadow clock, the first portable clock, was invented.

_____ People used hourglasses.

_____ Christiaan Huygens invented a pendulum clock.

_____ The first mechanical clocks appeared in public buildings in Italy.

_____ The Egyptians built obelisks to help them tell time.

Reading for Details

Answer the following questions about the reading. Use your own words and write complete sentences.

1. What were two problems with using an obelisk or a sundial to tell time?

   _____

   _____

   _____

2. What were two problems with water clocks?

   _____

   _____

   _____

3. Why do we have leap years?

   _____

   _____

   _____

Discussion

Talk about these questions in a small group.

1. When is it important to be on time? How important is it?
2. If a friend is supposed to meet you, but he or she is late, how long are you likely to wait?
3. Although we need international agreement on what time it is, not everyone marks time by the same calendar. What examples can you list of calendars used by various cultures? What do you know about each one?

Using New Words

Work with a partner. Take turns asking for and giving information. Then tell the class something about your partner.

1. Name something you usually have in your **pockets**.
2. Name something **high-tech** that you would like to own.
3. Name something you own that isn't easily **portable**.
4. Name all the kinds of **transportation** you have ever used.
5. Name a time in your life when you took a big **step**.

Writing

Choose a topic. Write a paragraph.

1. There are many popular sayings about time in English— for example, "Time is money" and "Time flies when you're having fun." Give your opinion of one of these sayings, or explain a saying from your first language that refers to time.

2. Choose a topic from **Discussion** above.

CHAPTER 22

Out with the Old, In with the New?

Writing in Chinese

GETTING READY TO READ

Read the questions. Check (✔) your answers. Then find out how your classmates answered the questions, and write the numbers in the chart.

¹a calculator

Questions	Class Survey Results
1. Did you use a calculator¹ in school when you were young? ❑ Yes ❑ No	_____ out of _____ people used calculators.
2. Did you spend much time in school practicing your handwriting when you were a child? ❑ Yes ❑ No	_____ out of _____ people worked hard on their handwriting.
3. Which statement is most true for you? ❑ I prefer to write by hand. ❑ I prefer to write on a computer.	_____ by hand _____ on a computer

READING

Look at the words and picture next to the reading. Then read.

Out with the Old, In with the New?

1   Modern technology is causing changes in our lives that have some people worried. Everyone agrees that new inventions have made life easier, but perhaps we need to ask, "Are we losing something along the way?"

2   Jack Riley is a fifth-grade student in Vancouver, Canada, and he is **annoyed**. His teacher has just said, "No more calculators in math class." Jack likes using a calculator to add, **subtract**, **multiply**, or divide, but his teacher is worried about her students' basic math skills. She wants them doing more math in their heads and on paper. She recently read about a study on the math skills of Canadian college students. Some of the students had lived and studied all their lives in Canada, while others had come to Canada from schools in China. The researchers found that the Chinese students were quicker at doing simple math problems and far better at doing **complex** ones. They also learned that the Chinese students had used calculators much less often during their early school years than the Canadians had. Jack's teacher has also read the report from the Third International Mathematics and Science Study (1999). According to this study, Canadian students are not keeping up with students from Japan, Korea, Singapore, or England. Jack's teacher **blames** technology.

3   Kate Gladstone of Albany, New York, has some similar feelings about technology. Gladstone is "the Handwriting Repairwoman." She helps people **improve** their handwriting so that others can read it better, and sometimes so that they can read it themselves. Businesses have asked her to work with their employees, and many doctors have taken her courses. People in the United States often **make fun of** doctors' bad handwriting, but Gladstone says it is nothing to laugh about. "We've got to be aware that handwriting is important," she says. Doctors have to write clear prescriptions[1] because their patients' lives may depend on them. Most of us have to be able to write notes to co-workers,[2] **fill out** forms, and write addresses that the post office can read. Gladstone

[1] a *prescription* = a doctor's written order for a specific medicine for a sick person

[2] *co-workers* = people who work together

continued

says that too many people never learned to write clearly in school, and too many people think it does not matter anymore. She feels that in the age of computers, handwriting is not getting the attention it **deserves**.

4   Li You lives in the city of Yangshuo in Guangxi, China. About eight years ago, he started using a computer to do word processing[3] in Chinese. Soon afterward, his memory for writing Chinese characters[4] by hand began to fail. He would pick up a pen and be unable to write something that he had learned as a child. Many of his friends have had the same problem. They used to be able to write thousands of characters. Now they often joke about how they try to write a character but cannot remember how to form it. At the computer, Li can easily **type** what he wants to say, so he is not worried. He does 95% of his writing at the computer now, and he says, "I can go for a month without picking up a pen." However, some people have a different view of the situation. "A long time ago, we all wrote much better," says Ye Zi, who works with Li. He says, "It's a cultural **loss**."

5   Are computers and calculators **robbing** people of **valuable** skills? Some people think so. Others say such questions just show that some of us cannot deal with change.

6   Jack's teacher thinks that students lose something when they depend on calculators, but other math teachers disagree. Kate Gladstone talks about the importance of handwriting, but she uses e-mail, too. Among writers of Chinese, opinions **vary** on the old way versus[5] the new. Some remember that until the 1900s, the brush—not the pen—was the **traditional** tool for writing Chinese, and writing was something that few people knew how to do. The pen replaced the brush because it was easier to use and carry around. Many people did not like this new development, but as the pen became more popular, it helped more people learn to write. We cannot avoid change, says Ming Zhou, a Microsoft researcher in Beijing. "It's just the way it is." He says the modern way is always to do things faster. "When culture and speed come into **conflict**, speed wins."

Kate Gladstone was quoted in "Why Farhad Can't Write" by Farhad Manjoo, August 16, 2000, <http:www.wired.com>. Li You, Ye Zi, and Ming Zhou were quoted in "In China, Computer Use Erodes Traditional Handwriting, Stirring a Cultural Debate" by Jennifer Lee, February 1, 2001, <http:www.nytimes.com>.

[3] *word processing* = the use of a computer and certain software to write

[4] the Chinese *character* for "Life"

[5] *versus* = (also *vs.*) as compared with, as opposed to

Quick Comprehension Check

Read these sentences. Circle T (true) or F (false).

1. All the people described in the reading feel the same way about technology.   T   F

2. Some people think the use of calculators hurts children's math skills.   T   F

3. A study was done in Canada on the math skills of college students.   T   F

4. According to the reading, handwriting does not matter anymore.   T   F

5. Some writers in China are forgetting how to write Chinese characters with a pen.   T   F

6. Some people worry about losing the old ways, and some do not.   T   F

EXPLORING VOCABULARY

Thinking about the Vocabulary

Which target words and phrases are new to you? Circle them here and in the reading. Then read "Out with the Old, In with the New?" again. Look at the context of each new word and phrase. Can you guess the meaning?

Target Words and Phrases			
annoyed (2)	blames (2)	deserves (3)	valuable (5)
subtract (2)	improve (3)	type (4)	vary (6)
multiply (2)	make fun of (3)	loss (4)	traditional (6)
complex (2)	fill out (3)	robbing (5)	conflict (6)

Using the Vocabulary

 A These sentences are **about the reading**. Complete them with the words and phrases in the box.

annoyed	blames	complex	conflict	deserves	loss
make fun of	robs	traditional	valuable	vary	

1. Jack Riley is a little angry with his teacher. He is _____ about her new rule.

2. The Chinese students in the study were better than the Canadians at doing _____ math problems. These were difficult problems with many parts or steps.

3. Jack's teacher thinks technology is responsible for the Canadian students' poor scores on math tests. She _____ technology.

4. People in the United States often joke that no one can read what doctors write. They _____ doctors' handwriting.

5. Kate Gladstone thinks that the teaching of handwriting should receive more attention in schools. It _____ more attention, she says.

6. Ye Zi believes that the Chinese culture loses something when people forget how to write characters. "It's a cultural _____."

7. Are computers and calculators taking something away from us? Some people think technology _____ people of skills they need.

8. Some skills are very useful. They are worth a lot. They are _____.

9. Not all writers of Chinese have the same opinion. Opinions _____ from one person to the next.

10. The brush was the tool used by Chinese writers for a very, very long time. It was the _____ tool. The computer is a modern tool.

11. Culture and speed have come into _____. This means that a situation has developed in which people have to choose between opposite sides.

B These sentences use the target words and phrases **in new contexts.** Complete them with the words and phrases in the box.

annoyed	blamed	complex	conflict	deserve	losses
make fun of	robbed	traditional	valuable	vary	

1. Because he is the slowest runner, the other boys laugh at him and _____ him.

2. Two people doing equal work _____ equal pay.

3. The team has a record of six wins, no _____, and one tie.

4. I was _____ with my brother for not giving me the message.

5. Can the police prove that he is the one who _____ the store?

6. Do you understand the political situation? It's fairly _____.

7. Her band plays both _____ songs that everyone knows and new ones that she writes herself.

8. We hope the _____ between the two nations does not develop into a war.

9. Schools across the state _____ in what and how they teach.

10. When the artist became famous, his paintings became more _____.

11. His parents _____ him for the broken window, but it was actually his sister who did it.

C **Read these sentences. Write the boldfaced target words or phrases next to their definitions.**

a. When you **subtract** 20 from 30, you get 10.

b. When you **multiply** 20 times 30, you get 600.

c. You can **improve** your skills with practice.

d. You have to **fill out** this form to apply for the job.

e. My secretary can **type** over 100 words per minute.

Target Words/Phrases	Definitions
1. _____	= make something better
2. _____	= write using a typewriter[1] or computer keyboard
3. _____	= add a number to itself a specific number of times
4. _____	= take a number or an amount from another number or amount
5. _____	= write all the necessary information in the spaces provided on a form

[1] a *typewriter*

Building on the Vocabulary

Studying Word Grammar

The verb *rob* and the verb *steal* have similar meanings, but they are used differently.

- Someone robs a person or a company: *He robbed a bank.*
- Someone steals a thing (from a person or company): *He stole money from the bank.*

Write two sentences. Use *rob* and *steal*.

1. _____

2. _____

DEVELOPING YOUR SKILLS

Comparing and Contrasting

Use information from the reading to complete each diagram below. What do the people have in common? How do they differ?

1. The Canadian study:

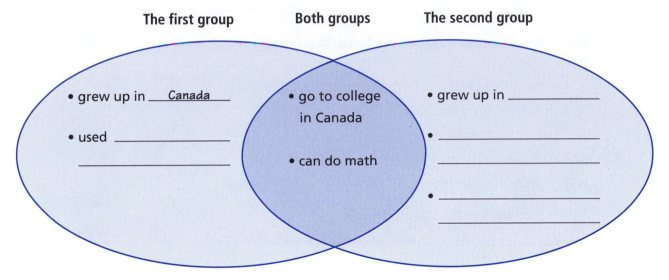

The first group   Both groups   The second group

- grew up in ___Canada___

- used _____

  _____

- go to college in Canada

- can do math

- grew up in _____

- _____

  _____

- _____

  _____

2. Li You and Ye Zi:

Li You   Both   Ye Zi

- thinks _____

  _____

  _____

- live in China

- can _____

- can _____

- thinks _____

  _____

  _____

Reading Between the Lines

These are inference questions. The answers to these questions are not given in the reading, but you can answer them if you understand the reading.

1. What does Jack's teacher believe about calculators? _____

   _____

   _____

2. What does Kate Gladstone want schools to do? _____

   _____

   _____

3. What would Ye Zi probably want his children to learn in school? _____

   _____

   _____

Summarizing

On a piece of paper, write a summary of "Out with the Old, In with the New?" Begin with a statement of the main idea. Then give three examples from the reading.

Sharing Opinions

Talk about the following opinions in a small group. Tell why you agree or disagree.

Opinion 1	Children need to spend a lot of time in school developing good handwriting.
Opinion 2	Children in school should spend more time learning to write on a computer than learning to write by hand.
Opinion 3	Children should not waste schooltime practicing handwriting or typing. In the future, we will speak to computers and they will do any necessary writing for us.

Using New Words

Work with a partner. Choose five target words or phrases from the list on page 209. On a piece of paper, use each word or phrase in a sentence.

Writing

Choose a topic. Write a paragraph.

1. Think of a tradition that has changed in your country in recent years. Describe the change and give your opinion of it.
2. Some people love new technology, others aren't interested in it, and some are afraid of it. What about you? What is your relationship with modern technology? Give an example from your life.

CHAPTER 23

Appropriate Technologies

Keeping vegetables fresh in a cooler made from two clay pots with wet sand in between*

Talk with a partner or in a small group.

1. What percentage of the people in the world do you think have no electricity?
   a. less than 10%   **b.** about 18%   **c.** about 33%

2. Do you know the phrases *developed countries* and *developing countries*? Read the definitions and list some examples of each.

   developed countries = rich countries with many industries, comfortable living for most people, and (usually) governments chosen by the people.

   Examples: _____

   developing countries = poor countries without much industry that are working to improve their people's lives.

   Examples: _____

* Developed by Mohammed Bah Abba of Nigeria for use in hot, dry places with no electricity

READING

Look at the words and pictures next to the reading. Then read.

Appropriate Technologies

1   You are probably reading this book in a developed country. So when you hear the word *technology,* you are likely to think of computers, high-tech phones, cars, and so on. Those of us who live in such countries can look forward to new **models** each year that may be even better. Modern technology has made life in developed countries much easier. Technology can make life easier in developing countries, too, but it has to be technology of another kind because the needs in such countries are very different. About two billion people—one-third of the people on Earth—do not even have electricity. What they need is technology that is **appropriate** for their situations, technology that will help them meet basic needs for food, water, clothes, housing, health services, and ways to make a living.

2   The **term** *appropriate technologies* means types of technology that:

- use materials available in the local area.
- can be understood, built, and **repaired** by the people who use them.
- bring communities together to **solve** local problems.

3   Some appropriate technologies are beautifully simple. For example, a project in Sri Lanka is using sunlight to make drinking water safe. Clear bottles are filled with water and placed in the sun for six hours. That is usually enough time for the sun to **heat** the water and kill germs.[1] If the weather is cool or cloudy, it takes two days. This **method** has already been proven to help people stay healthier.

4   Amy Smith is an inventor with a passion[2] for designing appropriate technologies. Smith studied engineering at MIT, the Massachusetts Institute of Technology (in the United States), and then spent four years in Botswana, in **southern** Africa. She taught math, science, and English there, and she trained farmers in beekeeping (looking after bees and getting honey[3] from them). In Botswana, she realized that she could help people more by using her skills as an engineer. Smith said, "The longer I was there, the more I realized there were **plenty** of inventions that could improve the quality of life."

continued

[1] *germs* = very small living things that can make a person sick

[2] a *passion* = a strong love

[3] Bees produce *honey.*

5 So Smith went back to MIT and started working on low-tech inventions. Her first great invention was a screenless hammermill. A hammermill is a machine that grinds grain[4] into flour. Usually a hammermill needs a screen[5] to separate the flour from the unwanted parts of the grain. But screens often break, and they are hard to replace, so regular hammermills are not of much use in **rural** Africa. Women there often end up grinding grain by hand and spending hours each day to do it. Smith's invention does not need a screen. It is cheap to build, simple to use, easy to repair, and it does not use electricity. With this machine, a woman can grind as much grain in a minute as she used to do in an hour.

6 Smith's invention has been a great success in Africa, but some other good ideas have not done so well. In **northern** Ghana, another project designed to help women failed partly for cultural reasons. The women in this area do most of the farming, and they spend a lot of time and energy walking to and from their farms. Most of the time, they are carrying heavy **loads** on their heads. They are very much in need of a better way to transport farm products, tools, water, and so on. Because bicycles are popular in the region, a bicycle trailer seemed to be a good **solution** to the problem. The trailer was like a shopping cart[6] but had two wheels and was attached to the back of a bike. However, the idea did not work. For one thing, it is the men in northern Ghana, not the women, who own and ride bicycles. In addition, the type of bicycle offered to the women was a bicycle with a crossbar.[7] A woman wearing a dress, as is traditional there, cannot ride such a bicycle.

7 Amy Smith and others are trying to develop technologies that do not need a lot of energy, but most people agree that electricity would be valuable in developing countries. Electricity would improve education, allow greater communication, let doctors store medicines that must stay cold, and do much more. The **production** of electricity sometimes causes **pollution**, but creative engineers can find ways to produce it without destroying **the environment**, perhaps using the energy of the sun, wind, or water. Of course, the problems of developing nations cannot all be solved by thinkers like Amy Smith, but many can. As she says, "Technology isn't the only solution, but it can certainly be part of the solution."

Amy Smith was quoted in "MIT Grad Student Designs Low-Cost Solution for High-Tech African Problem" by Denise Brehm, November 29, 1999, <http://web.mit.edu/newsoffice> and in "Questions and Answers" March 2001, <http://alumweb.mit.edu/opendoor>.

[4] *grinds grain* = crushes the seeds of plants like corn or wheat between two hard, moving surfaces

[5] a *screen* = a wire net with holes that only very small things can pass through

[6] a *shopping cart*

[7] a bicycle with a *crossbar*

Quick Comprehension Check

Read these sentences. Circle T (true) or F (false).

1. Today, only a few people in the world are without electricity.   T   F
2. The same technology will not work everywhere in the world.   T   F
3. *Appropriate technologies* means the most modern, high-tech machines.   T   F
4. Amy Smith is an engineer and an inventor.   T   F
5. Culture can influence how people use or feel about new technology.   T   F
6. Electricity would not help developing countries.   T   F

EXPLORING VOCABULARY

Thinking about the Vocabulary

Which target words and phrases are new to you? Circle them here and in the reading. Then read "Appropriate Technologies" again. Look at the context of each new word and phrase. Can you guess the meaning?

Target Words and Phrases			
models (1)	**solve** (2)	**plenty** (4)	**solution** (6)
appropriate (1)	**heat** (3)	**rural** (5)	**production** (7)
term (2)	**method** (3)	**northern** (6)	**pollution** (7)
repaired (2)	**southern** (4)	**loads** (6)	**the environment** (7)

Using the Vocabulary

 These sentences are about the reading. What is the meaning of each **boldfaced** word or phrase? Circle a, b, or c.

1. Each year, carmakers produce new **models** of cars. *Models* means:

    a. customers   b. habits   c. certain types
                                                            or designs

2. Technology for use in developing countries should be easy to **repair**. *Repair* means:

    a. blame   b. fix   c. drip

3. When the people in a community share a problem, they need to work together to **solve** it. *Solve* a problem means:

    a. find an answer to it   b. make fun of it   c. encourage it

4. People in Sri Lanka are using sunlight to **heat** their water and kill germs. *Heat* something means:

   a. measure it
   b. keep up with it
   c. make it warm or hot

5. They have a simple **method** for making their drinking water safe. *Method* means:

   a. a planned way of doing something
   b. a conflict between two forces
   c. a bad habit

6. Amy Smith realized there were **plenty of** inventions needed in Africa. *Plenty of* something means an amount that is:

   a. small or limited
   b. enough or more than enough
   c. decreasing

7. There is little modern technology in **rural** Africa. *Rural* means relating to:

   a. country areas, not the city
   b. expensive goods
   c. high-tech inventions

8. Water power is often used in the **production** of electricity. The *production* of something means:

   a. the investment in it
   b. the explanation of it
   c. the process for making it

9. Clean ways to make electricity do not hurt **the environment**. *The environment* means:

   a. all our land, water, and air
   b. people's lifestyles
   c. types of transportation

B These sentences use the target words **in new contexts**. Complete them with the words in the box.

environment	heat	method	models	plenty
production	repair	rural	solve	

1. He lives on a farm in a quiet, _____ area.

2. The accident was so bad that they can't possibly _____ the car.

3. You can get a TV at SuperBuy. There are lots of _____ to choose from.

4. I like her _____ of cooking rice. It has just a few, simple steps.

5. There's no need to rush—we have _____ of time.

6. He thinks money will _____ all his problems.

7. They burn wood to _____ their house.

8. The industry had to stop using chemicals that were bad for the

   _____.

9. Demand for the game was high, so the company increased

   _____.

C Read each definition and look at the paragraph number in parentheses ( ). Look back at the reading to **find the target word** for each definition. Write it in the chart.

Definition	Target Word
1. right for a certain purpose, situation, or time (1)	
2. a word with a specific meaning, especially in science or technology (2)	
3. in the south of an area, a state, a country, etc. (4)	
4. in the north of an area, a state, a country, etc. (6)	
5. amounts that are carried by a person, animal, truck, etc. (6)	
6. a way of solving a problem or dealing with a difficult situation (6)	
7. dangerous amounts of dirt or chemicals in the air, water, or soil (7)	

Building on the Vocabulary

Studying Word Grammar

The word *technology* can be:

- a noncount noun: *New technology is exciting.*
- a count noun, oft en plural: *Appropriate technologies are simple to use.* When it is plural, it means "types of technology."

Other nouns that are usually noncount, such as *fruit* and *cheese,* may also have a plural form meaning "types of."

   Eat plenty of *fruits* and vegetables. = Eat plenty of types of fruits and vegetables.

   My favorite *cheeses* come from France. = My favorite types of cheese come from France.

Circle the plural form when the noun means "types of." Circle the noncount form when it does not.

1. Some (food/foods) will affect the brain immediately; others won't.
2. Please give the cat her (food/foods).
3. They sell a variety of (coffee/coffees) from Latin America.
4. I'll have a cup of (coffee/coffees), please.
5. I use (shampoo/shampoos) to wash my hair.
6. The supermarket has lots of different (shampoo/shampoos).

DEVELOPING YOUR SKILLS

Understanding Cause and Effect

A Complete each sentence about the reading.

1. The technology needs of developing countries are different from those of developed nations because _____
   _____.

2. People in Sri Lanka put bottles of water in the sun because _____
   _____.

3. Amy Smith's invention is a good example of an appropriate technology because _____
   _____.

4. The women in Ghana did not use the bicycle trailers because _____
   _____.

B These are inference questions. The answers to these questions are not given in the reading, but you can answer them if you understand the reading. Write complete sentences.

1. Why should appropriate technologies use materials available in the local area? <u>Materials available in the local area are easy to get and probably cost less than materials from far away.</u>

2. Why did the people in Sri Lanka have to use sunlight to heat their water?
   _____

3. Why did Amy Smith leave Africa? _____

4. Why have women in Africa welcomed the screenless hammermill? _____
   _____

Understanding and Using Supporting Details

Write two statements with details that support each of the general statements below.

1. Technology means different things to people depending on where they live.

    <u>To people in developed countries, technology means high-tech inventions like computers and cars.</u>

    <u>To people in developing countries, technology means ways to meet basic needs.</u>

2. Appropriate technologies do not depend on high-tech machines or processes.

    _____

    _____

    _____

3. Bringing electricity to developing countries could have both good and bad effects.

    _____

    _____

    _____

4. Technology can make people's lives easier.

    _____

    _____

    _____

Discussion

Work with a partner or in a small group.

1. Fill in the chart with examples of modern technology that you use. Write what people had to do before the invention of each type of technology.

Modern technology:	In the past:
1. dishwashers	People used to wash dishes by hand.
2.	
3.	
4.	
5.	

2. Consider each of the types of technology in your chart. Which ones would you miss the most and the least if you didn't have them? Why?

3. Amy Smith spent four years living and working in a rural area of a developing country. Do you know anyone who has done something like that? Would you like to do it yourself? Why or why not?

Using New Words

Work with a partner. Take turns asking for and giving information.

1. Describe some kind of clothing that is not **appropriate** for school.
2. Name two things people can do to protect **the environment**.
3. Name something you can't **repair** if it gets broken.
4. Name two things you can find in **rural** areas.
5. Name something you have **plenty** of.

Writing

Write a paragraph that relates to question 2 or 3 from Discussion above.

CHAPTER 24

Technology in Science Fiction

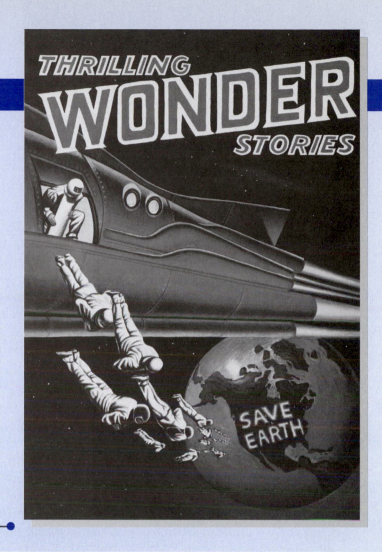

A science fiction magazine cover from 1941

GETTING READY TO READ

Talk with a partner or in a small group.

1. *Science fiction* means stories about future developments in science and technology and their effects on people. Sometimes these stories include travel by spaceship.[1] There have been many popular science fiction movies, such as *Star Wars*. What others can you name?

[1] *a spaceship*

2. **a.** Look at the magazine cover above. What is happening in the picture?

   b. An artist created this magazine cover in 1941. How well did the artist imagine the future? Explain.

READING

Look at the words and pictures next to the reading. Then read.

Technology in Science Fiction

1   Facts are pieces of information we know to be true. When we read history, we want to know the facts—what really happened. Fiction is the opposite. Writers of fiction **make up** stories, telling of people and events that come from the writer's **imagination**. Science fiction writers imagine not only people and events but, perhaps most importantly, technology. They often write about the effects of that technology on a person, a group, or **society**. These writers usually set their stories in the future. Some of them have **predicted** technology that seemed impossible at the time but really does exist today.

2   An Englishwoman, Mary Shelley, was one of the first writers of science fiction. In 1818, she wrote the book *Frankenstein*. It tells the story of a young scientist, Dr. Frankenstein, who wants to create a human life. He puts together parts of dead people's bodies, including—by mistake—the brain of a **criminal**, and then uses electricity to bring the creature[1] to life. But he cannot control the creature, and it kills him. Since then, the idea of a "mad scientist" (someone who tries to use science and technology to gain power) has been very popular in science fiction, especially in the movies.

3   In 1863, the French writer Jules Verne wrote the first of his many great science fiction **adventure** stories, *Cinq Semaines en Ballon* (*Five Weeks in a Balloon*). It is the story of three men traveling across Africa by hot air balloon.[2] Readers loved it, but many were **confused**: Was it fact or fiction? The story sounded unlikely, but the **style** of the writing and the **scientific** details made it seem true.

4   Later, Jules Verne wrote *Paris au Vingtième Siècle* (*Paris in the Twentieth Century*), a story he set 100 years into the future, in the 1960s. This story has **descriptions** of high-speed trains, gas-powered cars, calculators, skyscrapers,[3] and modern methods of communication, including fax machines. Verne imagined all these things at a time when **neither** he

continued

[1] a *creature* = a living thing (but not a plant)

[2] a *hot air balloon*

[3] a *skyscraper* = an extremely tall building

nor anyone in Paris had even a radio! In another book, *De la Terre à la Lune* (*From the Earth to the Moon*), he predicted that people would travel in **outer space** and walk on the moon, a prediction that came true on July 20, 1969. Verne even got some of the details right. Both in his book and in real life, there were three astronauts[4] making the **flight** to the moon, they **took off** from Florida, and they came down in the Pacific Ocean on their return.

5   Space travel continued to be a popular subject for science fiction in the twentieth **century**. The best writers based the science and technology in their stories on a real understanding of the science and technology of their time. Computers, robots,[5] and genetic engineering[6] all appeared in the pages of science fiction long before they appeared in the news.

6   The following quotation comes from a story by the great science fiction writer Isaac Asimov. He wrote these words in 1954. When you read them, remember that at that time, people had no computers in their homes. In fact, the few computers that existed were as big as some people's homes. In "The Fun They Had," Asimov describes a child of the future using a personal computer to learn math:

7   Margie went into the schoolroom. It was right next to her bedroom, and the mechanical teacher was on and waiting for her. . . .

8   The screen was lit up, and it said: "Today's arithmetic lesson is on the addition of proper fractions. Please insert yesterday's homework in the proper slot."

9   Margie did so with a sigh. She was thinking about the old schools they had when her grandfather's grandfather was a little boy. All the kids from the whole neighborhood came, laughing and shouting in the schoolyard, sitting together in the schoolroom. . . .

10   And the teachers were people. . . .

11   In 1954, readers probably found Asimov's story hard to believe. Fifty years later, his ideas don't seem so strange, do they? Maybe we should pay more attention to what science fiction writers are saying today about the world of tomorrow. But we should also remember that their predictions have been wrong more often than right. Here we are in the twenty-first century without flying cars, vacations on the moon, or robots cooking our dinner. And **in spite of** computers, people still do go to school.

Isaac Asimov's story "The Fun They Had" appears in *The Best of Isaac Asimov* (New York: Doubleday & Company, 1974), 153–155.

[4] an *astronaut* = someone who travels and works in outer space

[5] a *robot*

[6] *genetic engineering* = the science of changing the genes of living things

Quick Comprehension Check

Read these sentences. Circle T (true) or F (false).

1. Science fiction is often about the technology of the future.   T   F

2. People began writing science fiction in the 1900s.   T   F

3. A lot of science fiction is about people traveling in outer space.   T   F

4. Science fiction writers have imagined technology before it was invented.   T   F

5. A writer 50 years ago imagined computers replacing schools and teachers.   T   F

6. The predictions of science fiction writers are generally correct.   T   F

EXPLORING VOCABULARY

Thinking about the Vocabulary

Which target words and phrases are new to you? Circle them here and in the reading. Then read "Technology in Science Fiction" again. Look at the context of each new word and phrase. Can you guess the meaning?

Target Words and Phrases			
make up (1)	criminal (2)	scientific (3)	flight (4)
imagination (1)	adventure (3)	descriptions (4)	took off (4)
society (1)	confused (3)	neither . . . nor (4)	century (5)
predicted (1)	style (3)	outer space (4)	in spite of (11)

Using the Vocabulary

 These sentences are **about the reading**. Complete them with the words and phrases in the box.

adventure	century	confused	criminal	imagination
in spite of	make up	predicted	society	took off

1. Writers of history shouldn't invent anything, but writers of science fiction _____ almost everything.

2. The people and events in fiction come from the writer's _____ (his or her ability to think of new ideas or form mental pictures).

3. Science fiction often deals with the effects of future technology on
_____, meaning people in general.

4. Writers have imagined technologies of the future and described them
in their stories. They _____ that we would have these types
of technology.

5. By mistake, Dr. Frankenstein gave his creature the brain of a
_____, a person who broke the law and committed crimes.

6. Jules Verne's science fiction stories are full of _____. In other
words, they are about exciting experiences in which dangerous or unusual
things happen.

7. Readers of *Five Weeks in a Balloon* didn't know whether or not the story
was true. They didn't know what to think. They were _____.

8. In both the book *From the Earth to the Moon* and in real life, the astronauts
_____ from Florida. That is, their spaceships went up into the
air from Florida.

9. Science fiction books and movies were popular during the twentieth
_____ (the 100 years from 1900 to 2000).

10. Computers have not replaced teachers and classrooms. _____
computers (that is, even though computers exist), people still go to school.

B These sentences use the target words and phrases **in new contexts.**
Complete them with the words and phrases in the box.

adventure	century	confused	criminals	imaginations
in spite of	made up	predicted	society	took off

1. Jules Verne died in 1905. He died a _____ ago.

2. The actor didn't like his real name, so he _____ another.

3. Some people enjoy taking risks. They want exciting experiences. They go
looking for _____.

4. We _____ that they would solve the problem, and soon they did.

5. She told her students to use their _____ to find a solution.

6. It is the job of the police to catch _____.

7. _____ expects people to obey the law and respect the rights
of others.

8. The twins look so much alike that I can't be sure who's who. I get

_____.

9. He volunteered to do the job _____ the danger.

10. The plane _____ from Madrid several hours ago. In a little
while, it will land in Mexico City.

C Read these sentences. Write the **boldfaced** target words or phrases next to
their definitions.

a. I like the **style** of that car but not the color.

b. What time is the next **flight** to Paris?

c. H_2O is a **scientific** term for water.

d. He gave the police a **description** of the robber.

e. Sales have **neither** increased **nor** decreased. They have stayed exactly the
same.

f. He dreamed of traveling in **outer space**, of going to the moon and beyond.

Target Words/Phrases   Definitions

1. _____ = not (one person, thing, or action) and not
(another) either

2. _____ = the way something is made or done

3. _____ = relating to science or using its methods

4. _____ = a trip in a plane or space vehicle, or a plane
making a trip

5. _____ = the area outside Earth's air, also called
simply *space*

6. _____ = a piece of writing or speech giving details
of what someone or something is like

Building on the Vocabulary

Studying Word Grammar

After the phrase *in spite of,* you can use:

- a noun: *In spite of his injury, he stayed in the game and kept playing.*

- a pronoun: *The weather was bad, but we went out in spite of it.*

- a gerund (an *-ing* form of a verb used as a noun): *I went to class in spite of
feeling sick.*

Write three statements using *in spite of.*

1. _____

2. _____

3. _____

DEVELOPING YOUR SKILLS

Using Context Clues

The paragraphs in the reading from Asimov's story "The Fun They Had" contain words you may not know. Answer these questions about the story using the context to guess word meanings.

1. On the computer screen, Margie can read these words:

   Today's arithmetic lesson is on the addition of proper fractions.

   Which words are related to math? Circle them.

2. The computer tells Margie to "insert yesterday's homework in the proper slot." A slot is a long, narrow hole in a surface. We sometimes put letters into a mail slot or money into a coin slot.

   a. What is the meaning of *insert*? _____

   b. Do you think Margie does her homework on paper or on something

      else? Why? _____

      _____

3. Margie put her homework into the computer "with a sigh." These words show how she was feeling. Consider what Margie is thinking about. What do you think *a sigh* means? Check (✓) your answer.

   ❏ a big smile   ❏ an angry shout   ❏ a sad or tired sound

4. How do you think Margie feels about the way education has changed since

   the school days of her grandfather's grandfather? _____

   _____

Summarizing

On a piece of paper, write a one-paragraph summary of "Technology in Science Fiction." Include answers to the following questions:

- What does *science fiction* mean?
- Who was one of the first writers of science fiction?
- Who was Jules Verne?
- What were some of the things that Jules Verne accurately predicted in his stories?
- What happened with science fiction during the twentieth century?

Sharing Opinions

Answer the following questions. Then form a small group and find out the answers of the others in your group. Share the information about your group with the class.

1. Do you like to read science fiction:

    In your first language? ❑ Yes ❑ No

    In English? ❑ Yes ❑ No

2. Do you enjoy science fiction movies? ❑ Yes ❑ No ❑ Sometimes

    Examples of sci-fi movies you have seen: _____

    _____

3. What do you like or dislike about science fiction? _____

    _____

    _____

    _____

    _____

Using New Words

Work with a partner. Choose five target words or phrases from the list on page 226. On a piece of paper, use each word or phrase in a sentence.

Writing

Choose a topic. Write a paragraph.

1. Margie, the little girl in Asimov's story "The Fun They Had," knows a little about her grandfather's grandfather's life when he was a boy. What do you know, and what can you imagine, about the lives of any of your great-great-grandparents?

2. Become a science fiction writer! Imagine your life 30 years from now. Think especially about the technology you will use every day. Describe something from your daily life.

Wrap-up

REVIEWING VOCABULARY

Complete the phrase.

1. Write *methods of, a solution to,* or *steps in.*

   a. _____ a problem

   b. _____ a process

   c. _____ transportation

2. Write the verb *predict, repair,* or *type.*

   a. _____ a car

   b. _____ a letter

   c. _____ the future

3. Write the adjective *complex, rural,* or *valuable.*

   a. _____ jewelry

   b. a _____ situation

   c. a _____ area

4. Write the noun *applications, flour,* or *stories.*

   a. make up _____

   b. fill out _____

   c. measure _____

5. Write the adjective *accurate, equal,* or *modern.*

   a. an _____ report

   b. _____ amounts

   c. _____ society

6. Write the verb *rob, solve,* or *subtract.*

   a. _____ an amount

   b. _____ a problem

   c. _____ a bank

EXPANDING VOCABULARY

A In Unit 6, you learned *load, model,* and *step* as nouns and *blame, drip, heat,* and *repair* as verbs. In the following sentences, they are used differently because each of these words can be either a noun or a verb. Fill in the correct word. Is it a noun or a verb? Circle the answer.

1. My car is in need of _____repair_____. (*n.*/*v.*)
2. Our bags are all packed. Let's _____ them into the car. (*n./v.*)
3. I cleaned up a _____ of paint that fell on the floor. (*n./v.*)
4. They asked everyone standing in line to _____ to one side. (*n./v.*)
5. Whenever anything goes wrong, he gets the _____. (*n./v.*)
6. They go to the mountains to get away from the summer _____. (*n./v.*)
7. She put on the dress she bought to _____ it for her friend. (*n./v.*)

B On a piece of paper, write seven sentences with the words from Part A. Use the verbs as nouns and the nouns as verbs.

Example: My cousin can repair his own car.

C Sometimes an adjective forms its **antonym** (a word with the opposite meaning) by adding a prefix. For example:

| accurate—inaccurate | appropriate—inappropriate | equal—unequal |

Sometimes the antonym of an adjective is a different word. For example:

| high-tech—low-tech | northern—southern | rural—urban | valuable—worthless |

Use one word from each pair of adjectives to complete the sentences.

1. You can't wear that shirt to your job interview! It's _____.
2. The report was full of mistakes. It was highly _____.
3. The car was in such poor repair that it was almost _____.
4. North America, Europe, and most of Asia are in the _____ hemisphere.
5. There are many people, businesses, and big buildings in _____ areas.
6. My favorite method of writing is fairly _____—I use a pencil.
7. I broke the candy bar into two _____ parts and gave her the bigger one.

PLAYING WITH WORDS

There are 13 target words from Unit 6 in this puzzle. The words go across
(→) and down (↓). Find the words and circle them. Then use them to
complete the sentences below.

```
X  K  Q  P  O  R  T  A  B  L  E
A  C  O  N  F  U  S  E  D  O  Z
D  O  P  L  E  N  T  Y  E  S  X
V  N  P  W  X  Z  W  K  S  S  M
E  S  X  S  S  T  Y  L  E  X  P
N  T  M  Q  Z  K  V  Z  R  Z  O
T  A  Z  I  M  P  R  O  V  E  C
U  N  X  Z  M  X  K  X  E  Q  K
R  T  C  E  N  T  U  R  Y  Y  E
E  N  V  I  R  O  N  M  E  N  T
L  P  O  L  L  U  T  I  O  N  S
```

1. He's always traveling to exciting places. He loves _____adventure_____.

2. We are living in the 21st _____.

3. You can easily move a _____ TV.

4. Cars are bad for the _____.

5. No one can swim in that lake anymore. There's too much

   _____.

6. She got her hair cut in a new _____.

7. Your boss doesn't pay you enough. You _____ more.

8. Bring your friends to eat with us—we have _____ of food.

9. Living near the airport, they have the _____ sound of planes
   overhead.

10. I didn't understand what was happening. I felt _____.

11. I want to be a better player. How can I _____ my skills?

12. When my friend moved away, I felt a great sense of _____.

13. I put my hands in my _____ to keep them warm.

BUILDING DICTIONARY SKILLS

Look at the dictionary entries below. Then read each sentence and write the number of the meaning.

1. _____ a. I'm sorry, but I can't make it to the meeting tomorrow. I have a conflict.

   _____ b. The two partners ended up in constant conflict.

   _____ c. At first, the conflict was limited to just those two nations.

> **con·flict**[1] /'kɑn‚flɪkt/ n [C,U] **1** disagreement between people, groups, countries etc.: *The two groups have been in conflict with each other for years.* | *a conflict between father and son* | *conflicts over who owns the land* **2** a situation in which you have to choose between opposing things: *In a conflict between work and family, I would always choose my family.* **3** a war or fight in which weapons are used

2. _____ a. Do they treat their employees fairly?

   _____ b. It was a fairly traditional wedding.

> **fair·ly**[1] /'fɛrli/ adv **1** more than a little, but much less than very: *She speaks English fairly well.* **2** in a way that is honest or reasonable: *I felt that I hadn't been treated fairly.*

3. _____ a. The plane took off on time.

   _____ b. I took off my coat.

   _____ c. He was here a moment ago, but then he took off.

   _____ d. She took a month off after having her baby.

> **take off** phr v **1** [T take sth ↔ off] to remove something: *Your name has been taken off the list.* | *Take your shoes off in the house.* **2** [I] if an aircraft or space vehicle takes off, it rises into the air **3** [I] INFORMAL to leave a place: *We packed everything in the car and took off.* **4** [T take sth off] also **take off work** to not go to work for a period of time: *I'm taking some time off work to go to the wedding. . . .*

4. _____ a. The teacher varied the class, so we didn't get bored.

   _____ b. The weather varies a lot in the spring.

   _____ c. The movies he makes don't vary much, do they?

> **var·y** /'vɛri, 'væri/ v **1** [I] if several things of the same type vary, they are all different from each other: *Teaching methods vary greatly/enormously from school to school.* | *wines that vary in price/quality* **2** [I] to change often: *His moods seem to vary a lot.* **3** [T] to regularly change what you do or the way that you do it: *You need to vary your diet and get more exercise.*

Vocabulary Self-Test 2

Circle the letter of the word or phrase that best completes each sentence.

Example:

The radio isn't working. It needs new _____.

a. pills   c. batteries

b. nephews   d. degrees

1. I like exciting movies that are full of action and _____.

   a. adventure   c. flour

   b. service   d. investment

2. He needs a car, but he says he can't _____ one.

   a. beat   c. sail

   b. subtract   d. afford

3. The airplane was invented more than a _____ ago.

   a. flight   c. model

   b. century   d. space

4. The boss _____ me whenever anything goes wrong.

   a. robs   c. predicts

   b. blames   d. bakes

5. She left school at a young age. She didn't go _____ eighth grade.

   a. beyond   c. throughout

   b. within   d. besides

6. Those flowers do not need water. They are not real. They are _____.

   a. foreign   c. portable

   b. appropriate   d. artificial

7. Your heart is inside your _____.

   a. chest   c. market

   b. dust   d. lifestyle

8. They _____ money from the bank to buy their house.

    a. provided   **c.** borrowed

    b. attached   **d.** designed

9. We divided the bill so that we all paid _____ amounts.

    a. southern   **c.** equal

    b. mental   **d.** rural

10. Let's _____ a date for our next meeting.

    a. set   **c.** heat

    b. rent   **d.** blow

11. The two brothers think alike. They hold the same _____ on most things.

    a. sales   **c.** pockets

    b. firms   **d.** views

12. The company produces cars of high _____, so of course they are expensive.

    a. risk   **c.** production

    b. crime   **d.** quality

13. _____ the long trip and the late hour, the children didn't seem tired.

    a. Whatever   **c.** In spite of

    b. Since   **d.** Therefore

14. You have worked hard. You _____ some time off.

    a. appear   **c.** flow

    b. deserve   **d.** treat

15. If he practices, he will _____.

    a. prove   **c.** improve

    b. solve   **d.** invest

16. The reporters took notes on the _____ parts of the president's speech.

    a. key   **c.** such

    b. worth   **d.** aware

17. Drive slowly—the road is in bad _____.

    a. condition   **c.** pollution

    b. description   **d.** operation

18. Their research led to new _____ in medical care for patients with burns.

   a. loads   **c.** limits
   b. developments   **d.** surfaces

19. Who _____ your cat when you are away?

   a. thinks over   **c.** looks after
   b. fills out   **d.** deals in

20. He goes to all the games, so it isn't _____ that he would miss this one.

   a. scientific   **c.** huge
   b. valuable   **d.** likely

21. She is afraid of losing her job. She has little job _____.

   a. industry   **c.** injury
   b. society   **d.** security

22. Farmers are in a bad _____ after ten weeks of no rain.

   a. trade   **c.** situation
   b. material   **d.** method

23. I go to my grandfather for advice. He has always had a _____ influence on my life.

   a. recent   **c.** political
   b. confused   **d.** major

24. Everything around us is part of our _____.

   a. shadow   **c.** environment
   b. flight   **d.** term

25. His new haircut didn't look good, so his brothers _____ it.

   a. kept up with   **c.** took over
   b. looked into   **d.** made fun of

26. We don't know what will happen. The future is _____.

   a. plain   **c.** normal
   b. uncertain   **d.** political

27. A person who shops in a store is a _____.

   a. customer   **c.** criminal
   b. director   **d.** officer

28. You can both come in our car. We have _____ of room.

    a. none   c. fairly

    b. plenty   d. possibly

29. I cleaned out my notebook and _____ old papers I did not need.

    a. got to know   c. set up

    b. made up   d. got rid of

30. Computers did not _____ 100 years ago.

    a. spread   **c. exist**

    b. demand   d. encourage

31. The students _____ a lot of money at their summer jobs.

    a. repaired   c. measured

    b. doubled   d. earned

32. You don't have to do that. It isn't _____.

    a. similar   c. further

    b. necessary   d. annoyed

33. Water, oil, and juice are all _____.

    a. liquids   c. containers

    b. rules   d. processes

34. What is the first _____ in finding a job?

    a. loss   c. ad

    b. step   d. nation

35. I need to _____ my closet so that I can find things easily.

    a. multiply   c. organize

    b. block   d. drip

36. She has a small business with fewer than 20 full-time _____.

    a. nieces   c. volunteers

    b. employees   d. criminals

See the Answer Key on page 239.

Vocabulary Self-Tests Answer Key

Below are the answers to the vocabulary self-tests. Check your answers, and then review any words you did not remember. You can look up words in the index on the next three pages. Then go back to the readings and exercises to find the words. Use your dictionary as needed.

Vocabulary Self-Test 1 (Units 1–3; pages 115–118)

1. d	10. d	19. a	28. a
2. b	11. c	20. a	29. c
3. d	12. d	21. b	30. b
4. c	13. b	22. b	31. d
5. d	14. a	23. a	32. d
6. d	15. b	24. d	33. a
7. a	16. a	25. c	34. b
8. b	17. b	26. c	35. c
9. c	18. a	27. c	36. c

Vocabulary Self-Test 2 (Units 4–6; pages 235–238)

1. a	10. a	19. c	28. b
2. d	11. d	20. d	29. d
3. b	12. d	21. d	30. c
4. b	13. c	22. c	31. d
5. a	14. b	23. d	32. b
6. d	15. c	24. c	33. a
7. a	16. a	25. d	34. b
8. c	17. a	26. b	35. c
9. c	18. b	27. a	36. b

INDEX TO TARGET WORDS AND PHRASES